LESSONS
ON BECOMING

*52 WEEKLY INSPIRATIONS & REFLECTIONS ON
HOW TO BECOME THE SLP YOU WERE MEANT TO BE*

MATTIE MURREY TEGELS

MA, CCC-SLP, CPC, CLSC

Published by GWN PUBLISHING, LLC
Website: www.GWNPublishing.com

Editor: Layne Pratt

Cover Design By: Aaron Hill

ISBN Paperback 978-1-959608-08-0
ISBN EBook 978-1-959608-09-7

DEDICATION

This book is dedicated to my graduate students, my Fresh SLP friends, and my Badass SLP friends for whom this book is written. May you continue to lean into the dreams you had when you first started grad school and never lose your big WHY.

Here's to making a difference!

Foreword

"

SLPs, it isn't too late to chase that dream. To bring joy, friendships, and fun back into our profession. We don't have to be each other's biggest competition. Let's try, instead, to be each other's biggest inspiration. The future of the profession is ours -- let's ensure it lives up to our wildest dreams, and more. - Mattie Murrey Tegels

Five minutes after meeting Mattie, her passion for the field of speech-language pathology (and more specifically her passion for the PEOPLE in this profession) was evident to me. As colleagues in a university setting, Mattie and I have had many conversations about empowering emerging SLPs to develop as leaders in their circles of influence and the tension of excelling in a challenging profession while taking care of yourself.

Mattie is a soul whose kindness often masks the depth of her knowledge, compassion, and wisdom. In a university setting, Mattie brings not only 25+ years of clinical expertise, but masterful skill at offering capsules of wisdom in bite-sized formats. For example, in addition to her classroom and clinical teaching, Mattie created half-hour Touchdown meetings for graduate student clinicians each week focused on a topic of professional or personal development. The clear structure and exacting timeline of Touchdowns assured students that their time was well spent. The honest conversations helped unpack questions that might not be fully addressed in a classroom setting.

Mattie is an innovator and a lifelong learner with her primary focus on marking the path for newly minted and future SLPs. Her business has evolved from an educational resource site to include both personal and practical resources. It has been my privilege to co-present with Mattie on workplace well-being and to participate with her on Fresh SLP's Podcast, The Missing Link for SLPs: Fishbowl series offering honest conversation from 3 SLPs practicing in different settings.

Lessons on Becoming is a natural extension of the trajectory Mattie Murrey Tegels has charted in the world – bite-sized capsules of wisdom with the potential to influence enormous personal change. Simple, but not easy. It is my great privilege to recommend this book to new SLPs looking for advice in their career, seasoned SLPS looking to reexamine their journey, and non-SLPs seeking guidance to live life with intention.

Enjoy *Lessons on Becoming*!

-Janet Tilstra
Associate Professor & Graduate Director,
Communication Sciences & Disorders St Cloud State University

LESSONS
ON BECOMING

*52 WEEKLY INSPIRATIONS & REFLECTIONS ON
HOW TO BECOME THE SLP YOU WERE MEANT TO BE*

There are weeks throughout this book that are meant for specific holidays and events. Depending one when you start your reflections, you may find that you arrive on one of these weeks and it does not line up with the calendar. When this happens, please move on to the next week's reflection and come back to that dedicated reflection when the time or holiday has arrived.

You're Allowed to Begin Again

Don't be afraid to start over. This time, you are not starting from scratch. You are starting from experience.

Hi Fresh SLP,

It is funny how quickly we put ourselves into boxes that we think define us and our futures. Maybe we see ourselves as the funny one, the overachiever, the person who *always* knew that they wanted to be an SLP in a medical setting.

The labels and plans we set out for ourselves often feel useful at first --- and sometimes even make us feel proud --- but overtime, they can start to feel restrictive and inauthentic. After all, everyone grows and changes --- no one is the person today that they were ten years ago, or even last year. That's the beauty of life, and it is a **GOOD** thing.

Yet, as an SLP trying to find their way in our competitive profession, it can be SO comforting to cling desperately to these labels -- to the *path* we had mapped out for ourselves and our careers right out of graduate school. It can feel **SO** hard to acknowledge that we might need to make a change, or that a shift to our grand life plan might be required *(gasp!)*.

In moments like these, where you find yourself resisting a necessary change in your identity or path, I encourage you to reflect on this beautiful quote by Alex Elle:

"Trust yourself enough to shift, let go, uproot. Give yourself permission to shed who you used to be. You are allowed to start over and find new ways to bloom into your best self."

Fresh SLPs, read that again if you need to. Maybe even three times.

You are **ALLOWED** to grow and change! The person you used to be does not have to be the person you are tomorrow. You are allowed to change your mind, change your passions, change your career path, and change your **LIFE**.

The only person who can hold you back from making change is **YOU**.

So, as you embark on a new week, I encourage you to be aware of places in your life where you may be clinging to old labels, old habits, and old plans. And when you find them, I challenge you to break through them -- to be brave enough to replace them with new habits and plans that better serve the person *(and professional)* you want to be in the future.

Change is scary, but not as scary as living an inauthentic life. Go out and find the life you love -- it will be worth every risk.

Cheers,

Mattie

Courage to Ignite Change Challenge

> **"**
> *Challenges are gifts that force us to search for a new center of gravity. Don't fight them. Just find a new way to stand.*
> *~Oprah Winfrey*

Reflection Questions:

What boxes or labels have defined you over the course of your life?

How have they made you feel? Think? Operate?

How have they held you back or limited you?

What old labels/parts of yourself might you need to get brave enough to "shed"?

What do you want to create for your life in its place? Who do you want to be as you move ahead?

What will be required of you (bravery, skills, knowledge, etc.) to make this happen?

How will you know when you are successful in shifting your mindset?

The Company You Keep

"

The key is to keep company only with people who uplift you, whose presence call forth your best.
~Epictetus

Hi Fresh SLP,

Motivational speaker Jim Rohn famously said that you are the average of the five people you spend the most time with.

The first time I heard this idea, it stopped me in my tracks. I immediately began to think about my *top 5* people -- the people with whom I spend the majority of my time. I listed them all out on a piece of scrap paper, and began the humbling *(and slightly terrifying!)* work of considering who I am - and who I am becoming -- as a result of keeping their company.

Were they influencing me in positive ways?

Did their values align with mine?

Did they inspire and support me?

Was I becoming a **BETTER** version of myself by being around them?

This line of questioning brought into focus just how profoundly those around me leave their mark on my life in big and small ways -- for better, or for worse. As an entrepreneur committed to being brave, bold, and honest in my career, I quickly realized how having the wrong influences in my life could **REALLY** threaten my goals and dreams. I was told once that:

"If we cannot see the possibility of greatness, how can we dream it?"
~Lee Strasberg

With this *top 5* exercise behind me, I had never been more convinced of the truth in that quote. We simply must surround ourselves with role models -- the kinds of people we aspire to be -- to ensure we have the support and vision we need to see a clearer path toward our own greatness. Our very future depends on it, probably in more ways than we know at this moment.

So, this week, I challenge you to take stock of your Top 5 relationships! Think honestly about the impact they are having on your lives, and in what ways they are driving you toward -- or pulling you away from -- growing into the SLP, and human being, that you want to be.

If you find you need to make some changes, I wish you the bravery and courage you need to create those changes for yourself, despite the challenges that inevitably come with doing so. -- It won't be easy, but I promise it will be worth it.

Cheers,

Mattie

Courage to Ignite Change Challenge

"

Surround yourself with people that reflect who you want to be and how you want to feel. Energies are contagious.

~Rachel Wolchin

Reflection Questions:

List out your *top 5*-- the people with whom you spend the most time. Then consider:

How are these individuals influencing me?

Do their values align with mine? If not, where are the misalignments? If so, where are the alignments?

Did they inspire and support me to become a better version of myself?

What does this reflection make me think about my Top 5? Are they the people best positioned to help me reach my dreams?

If not, what changes do I need to make? How could I go about making those changes?

Is there anyone in my "top 5" that I want to spend less time with?

Is there anyone I want to invite into my "top 5" circle?

The Thing About Change

"

Embracing change is about adopting a growth mindset.
~Marco Marsans

Hi Fresh SLP,

Habits. They are hard to face, and when you get brave enough to look them in the eye, they are even harder to change. For the average person, it takes 66 days to form a new habit. That's 66 days in a row of waking up early to workout, or remembering to write in your gratitude journal, or practicing a new SLP-related skill before it becomes second nature. 66 days! It's no wonder many of us fail when trying to build new habits in our lives.

And yet, as new or transitioning SLPs, we can become impatient with ourselves when we aren't seeing the concrete changes we hope to see in our lives. Whether it is trying to eat healthier, practice more gratitude each day, or nail a new skill, we often wonder why we aren't seeing the changes we seek.

Well, Fresh SLPs, I suspect this quote from Tony Robbins might hold the answer for many of us:

"If you do what you've always done, you'll get what you've always gotten."~Tony Robbins

How many of us wake up day after day and do *(largely)* the same things? Engage in the same routines and behaviors? Spend time with the same people? Read the same things? Think the same way?

Friends, this quote brings into stark light the fact that change requires **DIFFERENT** behavior. Sometimes, radically different behavior. You can't get to a new destination without a new route, and you can't create change in your life without putting in the effort to build new habits. It is just that simple, and just that hard, all at the same time.

But are you capable of it? Absolutely.

This week, I encourage you to inventory your habits. Take 10 minutes to look at your day, from start to finish, and evaluate how you're spending your time.

• What habits do you hold?

• What do you do every single day? Why?

• Where are those habits leading you?

• Do you have goals for yourself that aren't served by these habits?

If you find you need to create new pathways toward your goals, I challenge you to identify **ONE** single habit you want to change, and work to do something **DIFFERENT** this week toward that goal.

No matter how small, the change will get you closer to your new destination, and give you the momentum and confidence you need to keep making changes. -- You are brave. You are capable. You are worthy.

The life you have now does not have to be the one you have forever. What will you do differently tomorrow to build a life you love?

Cheers,

Mattie

Courage to Ignite Change Challenge

> **"**
> *Change is inevitable. Growth is optional. ~John C. Maxwell*

Reflection Questions:

What habits do you hold?

_____

_____

_____

_____

_____

What do you do every single day, and why?

_____

_____

_____

_____

Where are those habits leading you?

Do you have goals that aren't served by those habits?

If so, where do you need to make changes?

_____

_____

_____

_____

_____

What is one thing you'll do differently tomorrow to build a life you love?

_____

_____

_____

_____

_____

Planting Your Seeds with Patience

> **"**
> *The day you plant the seed is not the day you eat the fruit.*
> *Be patient and stay the course.*
> *~Fabienne Fredrickson*

Hi Fresh SLP,

They say patience is a virtue, but if you're anything like me, patience can be hard to come by some days.

As SLPs, we are trained to move quickly, respond promptly to patient needs, and maintain a packed schedule. Often our day is filled with so much *hurry* and adrenaline that an unrealistic *(and unsustainable)* pace becomes the norm for us, and eventually, it begins to impact our expectations of ourselves and our careers.

Whether we are looking for our next job, CF placement, (or even our next significant other!), we expect that what we want will come quickly, don't we?! After all, we've put in the work. Shouldn't we see the reward?! Where is the payoff for the massive investment we're making?

In moments like these, when you're looking around in frustration wondering what you have to show for your hard work, or how much longer you'll have to *wait* to achieve your dreams, I encourage you to remember this quote:

"Don't judge each day by the harvest you reap, but by the seeds you plant." ~ Robert Lewis Stevenson

Fresh SLPs, hear this: your hard work is never in vain. Every single smile you share with a patient, every task you check off, every lesson you learn, is a seed being planted. It may not bloom instantly (wouldn't that be nice?!), but it is a part of your foundation. With time, nurturing and attention, those seeds will grow even **BEYOND** your wildest dreams -- I promise.

If you had told me ten years ago that I'd be leading the Fresh SLP community today, I'd never have believed it. But looking back, I see that -- all along -- even in the tiniest moments, I was planting seeds. Building relationships, gathering ideas, growing my confidence. I didn't know it yet, but Fresh SLP was just under the surface, ready to break free.

The same is true for you.

Keep planting your seeds with patience. Have faith they will grow into more than you could have ever dreamed. Your future is waiting for you.

Cheers,

Mattie

Courage to Ignite Change Challenge

"

Sometimes things aren't clear right away. That's where you need to be patient and persevere and see where things lead.
~Mary Pierce

Reflection Questions:

What seeds are you currently "planting with patience" in your life?

Which one are you the most proud of? Why?

What fruits do you hope these seeds will yield in time?

What new seeds do you need to start planting to set you up to achieve future goals?

How will you know when your seeds begin to bear fruit?

What does success look like to you?

Refreshing Your Goals and Dreams

> **"**
> *The future belongs to those who believe in the*
> *beauty of their dreams.*

Hi Fresh SLP,

I can't believe it is already February! Cheers to us for making it through the first months of the year. .

I have to admit that January proved to be a bit of a bumpier ride than I expected, and as the optimism and excitement that comes with a new year starts to fade, I find that this can be the exact moment in time where we *ALL* become vulnerable to losing a firm grip on our vision and goals.

You remember them, right?! Those bold, big dreams we talked about a month ago? The ones you were planning to share out loud with the world? The ones that set you on fire? Are they still driving you? Do they still feel within reach?

Look, friends. It can be *SO* easy to fall into complacency at this point in the year. To let old habits win. To decide that maybe, just maybe, those big goals and dreams might not be worth all the hard work and discipline that they require, after all. That it might just be easier and simpler to throw in the towel and live the way we always have.

And hey... if you're feeling that way today, that's OK. We've all been there. We are only human, and commitment to something new and something hard takes time and intentionality.

But if you *ARE* in that space, I challenge you. I challenge you to flip back to the pages in your notebook where you wrote down those goals. Read them again. Let them sink in. Let them fill you up! Let them remind you of all you already are, and all you can be.

Remind yourself that, "It always seems impossible until it is done." *(Nelson Mandela).*

Then, pick yourself up, and recommit. Rip those goals out of your notebook and post them on the refrigerator for all to see. Call up a friend and share with them the details of your dreams and plans. Ask them to be a support to you along the way. Remind yourself that nothing is impossible.

And if you're worried, like I often am, that you don't have what it takes to make it happen? I promise: you already have all you need within you.

Cheers,

Mattie

Courage to Ignite Change Challenge

"
Vision is everything.

Reflection Questions:

What goals have you set that you need to recommit to?

_____

_____

_____

_____

_____

What has prevented you from making progress toward them? *(mindsets, knowledge, resources, time, etc.)*

_____

_____

_____

_____

What are three concrete things you can do this week to help move you close to your goals?

How would your life be different if you reached those goals?

Why do they matter?

Chase the Dreams That Scare You

> **"**
> *Don't give up on your dreams, or your dreams will give up on you.*
> *~John Wooden*

Hi Fresh SLP,

Last week, I encouraged each of you to visualize your dreams, and then set **SMART** goals to help you reach them. But what about the dreams themselves? How do you decide on them? How do you know if they're right for you?

I'll start by sharing this quote that I've always loved:

"If your dreams don't scare you, they are too small."

I know from personal experience that it can be so tempting -- especially when we're doubting ourselves or feeling unsure of our potential -- to *downplay* our most precious dreams. To make them simpler or smaller, or even to hide them from others who we fear may doubt our chances of success.

But the thing about dreams is that they are meant to scare you! They are meant to be BIG. They are meant to live out in the world and be shared with others. It is in and through this sharing -- in this vulnerability -- that we give our dreams life and accountability. That we make them **REAL**.

So, I challenge you! Have you been brave enough in setting your goals for this year? Have you spoken them out loud? Have you shared them with others who can support you on your journey? If not, I promise you won't regret doing so.

Cheers to the big dreams that scare us just a bit,

Mattie

Courage to Ignite Change Challenge

> **"**
> *Character is the ability to carry out a good resolution long after the*
> *excitement of the moment has passed.*
> *~ Cavett Robert*

Reflection Questions:

What goals have you set out for the new year?

_____

_____

_____

_____

_____

Are they brave enough? Bold enough?

_____

_____

_____

_____

Have you shared them with others who can help hold you accountable? If not, when/how will you do this?

What changes do you hope to see in your life as a result of reaching these goals?

What makes them worth working towards?

Let the Tides Rise

"
The lowest ebb is the turn of the tide.
~Henry Wadsworth Longfellow

Hi Fresh SLP,

Winning is fun, isn't it?

In our context, winning can take lots of forms -- nailing a tough exam, landing a dream CF, watching a patient recover with our help, getting a promotion.

At the end of the day, it just feels **GOOD** to do our jobs well -- and that's normal! It is human nature to want to achieve and to find success. This thirst to win is part of what pushes us to be great in our roles!

And yet, life experience tells me that as a new or transitioning SLP -- especially if you are moving into a new CF or new full-time role -- winning simply isn't always in the cards.

It's a tough pill to swallow, I know. It was for me, too. For all of us control freaks, Type-A personalities, and over-achievers, the thought of *NOT* being successful right away can be crippling.

Almost crippling enough to make you quit. Or wish you hadn't started in the first place. I know, because I've been there.

But the thing is, as much as we might want to walk into day one of our new CF and nail our first evaluation, we might not. We might forget a step, or feel unsure of what to do next. We might feel in over our heads.

As much as we want to *prove* ourselves to our supervisor, we might find that we actually have a lot more to learn before we are ready to work independently. We might need way more support than we had expected.

And you know what? All of this is OK. It is how it is meant to be, in fact!

One of my favorite African Proverbs is that *"smooth seas do not create skillful sailors."*

Fresh SLPs, many of you are embarking on a powerful - yet challenging! - time in your career where the goal must be learning and growth, not perfection. Each challenge, each wave in the sea, is simply meant to teach you something new -- not just about how to be an excellent SLP, but sometimes, about how to be a better version of yourself.

So on day one of your CF *(or new job)* when you feel the waters rise, take a breath. Remember that each challenge will bring with it the opportunity to develop new skills, mindsets and relationships that will become added tools in your tool belt for the next time you encounter a similar challenge.

Remind yourself that *messing up* is OK. In fact, it is good, because it is a critical part of the learning process.

Is it easy to struggle? To feel like you're failing? To wonder if you have what it takes? Of course not. Is it a normal part of learning? Of growing your skill? Of honing your craft? Of becoming the SLP you were born to be?

Absolutely. And if that's the case?! I say bring on the waves.

Cheers to rocking the boat. It's always worth the reward.

Mattie

Courage to Ignite Change Challenge

"
Every inch of progress is won in struggle. ~ Katha Pollitt

Reflection Questions:

What has your orientation to failure been thus far in life?

How do you experience it and deal with it? Is it something you're used to? If so, where/how has it shown up for you in the past?

Where have you felt like you've failed in your journey as an SLP? What was that experience like for you?

How do you want to challenge yourself to think about moments of failure you may encounter in the future?

Write a self-affirming mantra below that you can recite to yourself in tough moments. *(Ex: I am learning. I am brave. This moment does not define me. I will be OK.)*

You Can't Pour from an Empty Cup

> **"**
> *Take time to do what makes your soul happy.*

Hi Fresh SLP,

If you're anything like me, stopping to take time for yourself can be tough. As SLPs, we are trained to think of and serve others at all times, often pushing our own needs aside and ignoring our body's natural cues to slow down and hit pause. We may not realize what is happening to us in the moment, but inevitably, this pace erodes not just our bodies, but also our minds and spirits.

I can recall with such clarity many sleepless nights of work and worry, especially early in my career, and I know many of you may be experiencing that same level of exhaustion as you transition from graduate school into your Clinical Fellowships this summer.

As we celebrate a day of rest and reflection this Memorial Day, I want to share a gentle but important reminder for all of us as SLPs:

Self-care is not self-indulgence, it is self-preservation.

This simple yet profound quote by Audre Lorde serves as a constant reminder to me that I can only support others when I have given myself the care, time and rest I need to be my best. After all, we all know it is impossible to pour from an empty cup.

So, in what ways are you hitting pause and finding a moment of rest this Memorial Day Weekend?

What might you need to change or shift in your day today to carve out time to make this happen?

My hope for you is that you're able to find at least one small way to fill up your cup today, and that you don't feel guilty about doing so for a single moment. Carving out time for self-care is the only way you can be the fullest version of yourself as you enter the rest of this week.

Your patients and colleagues deserve that -- and so do you.

Cheers,

Mattie

Courage to Ignite Change Challenge

Repeat as needed:

"
"I will remember to care for myself today."

Reflection Questions:

What are your needs right now? How aware are you of those needs?

In what ways are you meeting those needs and filling your cup?

In what ways are you falling short? Where are you feeling maxed out?

What would it take to more intentionally set aside the time, energy and resources to fill your cup?

In the space below, commit to 1-2 concrete changes you can make to your day/week - effective immediately! - to better meet your own needs. Make sure they are realistic and bite-sized so you can be successful and build from that success!

YOU Are the Person You Are Waiting For

"

Confidence is something you create when you believe in yourself.

Hi Fresh SLP,

A number of years ago, I read a quote that literally stopped me in my tracks:

"If the strongest blizzard starts with a snowflake, why can't you change the world?" - Unknown

Wow. Why can't I change the world?!?

I replayed this question over and over again in my mind, realizing that it was one I had never really considered before.

To be honest, as someone who is an expert in self-doubt, I always figured there must be someone else -- anyone else, really! -- who is better qualified to do the big, important stuff in life. Someone more experienced, more confident, more charming. After all, what could I possibly have to contribute that could be better than what they have to offer?

Fast forward a handful of years, and here I am watching the Fresh SLP community -- a vision I had held in my heart for so long -- come to life right before my eyes.

You see, at some point in my journey, I realized that the dream I had to create a community that was specifically designed to support new and transitioning was a dream all of my own! There wasn't anyone else out there who seemed to be

meeting the need in the way I had imagined, and I soon realized that the person best positioned to carry this vision to life wasn't someone else. It was me.

And what's more? It hit me like a ton of bricks that if I didn't do it -- if I got too scared to bring it to life -- it might never be.

Fresh SLPS, you are unique! Each dream, skill, passion, and talent is uniquely yours. It can't be duplicated, replaced, or diminished. If only I had been told that years ago, I may not have waited so long for someone else to come make my dream come true for me. I may have realized, a lot sooner than I did, that I was actually the person I was waiting for.

I'm not saying there aren't hard days. There are absolutely days where I wake up and doubt if I have what it takes, and if I'm really the right person to give the Fresh SLP community what it needs to thrive. But at the end of those days, I fight like heck to silence that voice, to give myself grace for letting it get the best of me, and to pick myself up and try again.

Watching this community grow, and seeing the ways you inspire and support one another, has been one of the greatest gifts and privileges of my lifetime. This week, I encourage you to consider what dreams you may be holding quietly in the silence of your hearts.

They might just be ready to fly.

Cheers,

Mattie

Courage to Ignite Change Challenge

"

You get in life what you have the courage to ask for.

Reflection Questions:

If you're being honest with yourself, what dreams might you be holding in the silence of your own heart?

What are the barriers (mental, financial, emotional, etc.) that prevent you from letting those dreams fly? What is it -- deep down -- that truly stops you?

What mindsets do you have about bringing dreams to life? What have you been taught or conditioned to believe/think/feel about dreaming?

What might it take to bring your own dreams to life?

What mindsets, knowledge, skills or resources would be required to get you started? Brainstorm a list below, and commit to taking action on a few to get you going in the right direction.

Enjoy the Beauty of Becoming

"
True beauty is really about being authentic and owning your uniqueness. ~ Kimberly Snyder

Hi Fresh SLP,

Waiting. Waiting can be tough.

I've been thinking a lot about how as new and transitioning SLPs, it can feel like we spend a lot of time waiting. Waiting for grad school to end, or for a CF or new role to begin. Waiting to make a move to a new place, to end a relationship, or to begin a new one. Waiting to figure out what the next step in our career might be.

Maybe, if we're being honest with ourselves, we're really just waiting for all the little pieces of our lives to finally - magically! - fall into place.

In these seasons of waiting and anticipation, it can be SO incredibly easy to want to speed up time. To jump ahead. To fast-forward and rush past all the baby steps and roadblocks "in your way" until you've finally "arrived" at your long-awaited destination. I get it. I've been there over the years -- in 1000 different ways. Personal and professional. Big and small. It's a feeling I know all too well. And when I find myself in this headspace, I try to reflect on this stunning quote by Mandy Hale:

"Trust the wait. Embrace the uncertainty. Enjoy the beauty of becoming. When nothing is certain, anything is possible."

Anything is possible! It was for me, and it is for you, too, Fresh SLPs.

Looking back on my career, I realize that there was so much joy and LIFE to be lived in those small moments that I tried to rush away. The ones that passed me by when I was too busy looking ahead and yearning for something else to notice and appreciate them. Lessons to learn, people to love, experiences to have, moments to cherish.

If I could turn back time and do it all again, I would SLOW DOWN and take a look around! I'd enjoy every step in my career -- even those "in between" times of uncertainty -- for the unique and valuable gifts they were offering. For the ways that those smaller, less "shiny" moments shaped and grew me in all the ways I needed.

If you find yourself in a time of transition and waiting, I challenge you to reframe your mindset this week. Remember that ultimately, each phase of your life -- even the seemingly insignificant ones -- builds you into the person you will become.

This very moment is deserving of your time, energy and attention. There are graces to be found all around you. Today.

What will you do with this moment?

Cheers,

Mattie

Courage to Ignite Change Challenge

> **"**
> *There's power in allowing yourself to be know and heard,*
> *in owning your unique story, in u sing your authentic voice.*
> *And there's grace in being willing to know and hear for others.*
> *This, for me, is how we become.*
> *~ Michelle Obama*

Reflection Questions:

Are you currently in a period of transition / waiting in your life? If so, what has that experience been like for you?

_____

_____

_____

_____

_____

What goals and hopes do you have your sights set on in the future?

_____

_____

What graces can you find around you in the present moment?

What people, places, relationships, things, and experiences surround you that are worthy of celebration and appreciation?

How might you work to more intentionally appreciate and enjoy them?

Just Bloom

> **"**
> *Bloom like a flower. Unfold your own beauty.~ Debasish Mridah*

Hi Fresh SLP,

Comparison is a funny thing. From the moment of our birth, it begins. Our doctors track our growth against what's "normal" beginning on the day we are born, and throughout our childhood. Our parents wait with baited breath for us to crawl, to walk, to talk -- often feeling overwhelmed by anxiety and worry if our cousin or the kid down the street reaches these milestones before us.

When we get to school, the comparisons continue. And what's worse?! We begin to be labeled based on those comparisons. We become the short one, the smart one, the shy one, or the chubby one. We start to form an identity around these labels, as if they are somehow indicative of our value and worth.

As new and transitioning SLPs, the comparison continues and intensifies. We are often compared to our peers, to others in our program, or even to those in our CF settings. We beat ourselves up over every grade, every piece of hard feedback, everything we feel that we aren't compared to the person next to us. And you know what?

All of this comparison isn't doing a single thing for us -- in fact, it is hurting us! It's hurting our confidence, and it's preventing us from appreciating our unique strengths. It's distracting us from connecting with our mentors and patients. It's preventing us from being the SLP -- and human being -- we were born to be.

So, the next time you find yourself tempted to look at the person next to you to see how you measure up, I encourage you to remember this beautiful quote by Zen Shin:

"A flower does not think of competing with the flower next to it. It just blooms."

It just blooms. Wow!

Fresh SLPs, what if you just bloomed?!? What if you pushed away all the noise, the insecurity, the comparison, and the doubt, and instead, gave yourself permission to be exactly who you were meant to be?

Without judgement? Without critique? Without comparison?

I have a feeling things would be different for you, and for all of us as SLPs, if only we had the bravery to do it.

Cheers to blooming,

Mattie

Courage to Ignite Change Challenge

"
The only person you should try to be better than is who you were yesterday.

Reflection Questions:

In what ways do you judge yourself? In what ways do you judge others?

What are some of the strengths, traits, and characteristics that make you, YOU?

What do others notice and appreciate in you / about you?

How can you leverage and reflect on those strengths in moments where you are

tempted to compare yourself to others?

What people, places, and spaces best embrace you without comparison or judgement? How can you spend more time leaning into those relationships and spaces?

What is one commitment you can make to yourself to allow you to "just bloom' without pressure or comparison?

You Either Win or You Learn

> **"**
> *You don't learn by following the rules. You learn by doing and falling over. ~ Richard Branson*

Hi Fresh SLP,

You are on my mind in a special way as we head into the summer season. Many of you are graduating, preparing to begin your CFs, or experiencing another pivotal moment of transition in your career as an SLP. Big things are happening, and it has been such a joy to witness each of you grow more fully into who you are meant to be!

While these moments of change and growth along your journey can be exciting, I know first-hand that they can also be incredibly stressful -- scary, even. I know the pressure you experience as new or transitioning SLPs is significant. I know it can sometimes feel crippling.

Will I impress my supervisor? Will I feel that I have enough support and supervision? Will I figure out how to create and stick to an effective schedule? Am I *REALLY* cut out for this?

If you find questions like these swirling around in your mind these days, know that you are not alone! Also know that the risk of failure you're feeling isn't as much of a threat as it seems to be in this moment. I promise.

One of my favorite quotes from Nelson Mandela is:

"I never lose. I either win, or I learn."

Many of you are entering a stage in your career where you'll experience the joy of winning almost daily! You'll nail a dysphagia evaluation during an observation by your supervisor, or you'll know just the right thing to say to reassure a worried patient and their family. And winning feels good! We all know that.

But in those harder moments? The ones where you aren't quite sure what to do next to treat a patient, or when you miss a step in an evaluation, or when you just aren't sure if you're up to the challenge? In those moments, you won't fail. You will **LEARN**.

You see, in very few cases is failure really an option. Most often, you're presented with an opportunity to learn. To grow. To stretch. To find out what you are really made of -- especially in the toughest moments. Especially when you're not sure you see a way forward.

This never-ending cycle of learning, growing and conquering is one of the sweetest and most rewarding joys we have as SLPs. What could possibly be better?!

Cheers to not fearing the fall,

Mattie

Courage to Ignite Change Challenge

"

Mistakes are a fact of life. It is the response to error that counts.
~ Nikki Giovanni

Reflection Questions:

In what ways have you been pushed to learn and grow lately in your role as an SLP?

_____

_____

_____

_____

_____

How have these moments of learning felt for you? In what ways do they challenge

you personally and professionally?

_____

_____

_____

_____

What is your orientation to growth and growth mindset?

Did you grow up in an environment where you were encouraged to change and grow? Where mistakes were accepted and embraced?

If so *(or if not!)*, how did that experience shape and inform you?

_____

_____

_____

_____

_____

What do you hope you can learn -- or unlearn -- about growth and failure as you move forward in your career as an SLP?

_____

_____

_____

_____

_____

Embracing Who We Are

"

Don't worry about what people think of you. Be who you are and say what you feel, because those who mind don't matter, and those who matter don't mind. ~ Bernard M. Baruch

Hi Fresh SLP,

"So tell me a bit about yourself!"

This is a request we get all the time as SLPs. We hear it from colleagues, potential bosses, professors and countless others. I suppose I should be used to it at this point, but I have to admit that hearing it from someone new still causes my heart to race just a bit.

You see, for me, it's not always easy to be honest and open with exactly who I am. While there are so many parts of me and my identity that I'm proud of, there are also parts that I'm less eager to share.

You know what I mean -- the parts that we try to dance around in conversation, or conveniently *forget* to mention when we introduce ourselves to someone new. The less pretty parts, the less popular parts, the less conventional parts. The ones that sting a bit just to think about, let alone share with the world.

However, as I've grown in my career and been faced with answering this question of "who I am" countless times, this quote by Brene Brown as given me the perspective I need to respond with just a touch more honesty:

"Authenticity is the daily practice of letting go of who we think we are supposed to be, and embracing who we are."

Letting go of anything is hard. Letting go of who we feel we are supposed to be is potentially the hardest thing of all.

With that said, being an SLP requires our authenticity! Our role demands that we be ourselves, even when it is challenging to do. Authenticity allows our patients to build the trust and connection with us that is needed for us to care for them. It allows our co-workers to understand how best to partner with us as teammates. It allows our bosses to know how best to support and grow us as professionals. Ultimately, authenticity is required for a fruitful career as an SLP.

So, the next time someone casually asks you to "tell them a bit" about who you are, I encourage you to pause for a moment to consider your response.

What might it take for you to open up a bit more than usual? To be a bit vulnerable? To tell more of the story? **YOUR** story. If you were willing to share with true authenticity, what might you end up gaining?

From personal experience, I promise you that the benefits outweigh the costs -- if only you're willing to be brave!

Cheers to letting go,

Mattie

Courage to Ignite Change Challenge

> **"**
> *Be yourself completely. To be yourself in a world that is constantly trying to make you something else is the greatest accomplishment.*
> *~ Ralph Waldo Emerson*

Reflection Questions:

How do you feel when someone asks you to *"tell them a bit"* about you?

What things do you typically share? Why?

What things do you typically leave out? Why?

What might it take to share more of your story?

What reward might you experience from being brave enough to do so?

What is one piece of your story that you want to start sharing more openly? Use the space below to jot down how you might talk about it to someone new.

Reclaiming Your Happiness

> **"**
> *Sometimes happiness is a feeling. Sometimes it's a decision.*

Hi Fresh SLP,

I've been thinking a lot recently about the concept of happiness. As new or transitioning SLPs, there can be a lot of pressure to feel *happy* and stay positive each day despite the many challenges that come with our role -- after all, some people would give anything to be where we are!

And yet, there is something elusive about happiness that makes it tricky to capture (and hold onto), despite our best intentions.

Someone wise once told me to try to "Be happy not because everything is good, but because you can see the good side in everything."

After thinking about it for a while, it became startlingly clear to me that I had been looking for happiness in all the wrong places! As it turns out, true happiness isn't something that comes or goes with luck or circumstances, or that you have to *find* and then try to hold onto for dear life *(we've all been there, haven't we?)*. It isn't even found when you *check the boxes* of your professional life -- when you finally graduate, or when you land your first job, or when you get a raise *(although those things will of course provide temporary moments of joy)*.

Real happiness - the kind that stays with you regardless *(and often in spite of!)* circumstances -- is internal and unconditional. It is found in your perspective on

life, and it is cultivated each and every day through your conscious decisions to see the good in all situations and in all people *(including yourself)* -- even when it is challenging to do so. This kind of unshakable happiness -- the real stuff! -- burns steadily within you, regardless of the inevitable challenges that will come your way, for a lifetime.

Friends, today I challenge you to reframe and reclaim your happiness as your responsibility! To push yourself to remember that true happiness is ultimately much more dependent on your choices than it is on your circumstances.

Does having that much ownership over your own happiness feel a bit scary? Maybe! It certainly did to me.

Is it worth putting in the work to intentionally choose, cultivate, and create your own happiness from within? Absolutely. It is the ultimate gift you can give to yourself, and one that can never, ever be taken away.

Cheers to a lifetime of the *real stuff,*

Mattie

Courage to Ignite Change Challenge

" Your life is too important to live life unsatisfied.

Reflection Questions:

How do you define happiness?

_____

_____

_____

_____

_____

What risk is there -- if any -- in defining happiness in this way?

_____

_____

_____

_____

What people, places, experiences, etc. currently bring you happiness?

How might you want to expand your understanding of happiness -- and how to attain it -- as you grow in your career?

What are the things that you feel will *truly* make you happy in this life?

How can you work towards those things today?

Is there anything *(or anyone)* you need to consider removing from your life in order to find more genuine happiness?

Giving Up What Weighs You Down

> "
> *The day I understood everything was the day I stopped trying to figure everything out. The day I knew peace was the day I let everything go. ~ C. JoyBell*

Hi Fresh SLP,

For me, the newness of spring often comes with a desire to create something new and different in my life. At these times, I often find myself stopping to take stock of my life, and looking with careful consideration and reflection at my victories, my losses, my progress, and yes, even my baggage.

It is through this process that I often realize how much heartache I am carrying around with me each and every day -- worries, fears, anxieties, past traumas, hard memories. If we aren't careful, the pains of life can pile up as fast and as high as the laundry. And the thing is? These burdens often prevent us from moving forward -- from creating the newness we seek.

Budda said:

"If you do what you've always done, you'll get what you've always gotten."

I don't know about you, but "giving up" what weighs me down isn't always as easy as it seems. First, we have to be self-aware enough to know what weighs us down in the first place! This requires us to find the time to think, to reflect, to journal, maybe even to seek counseling or outside support if needed. Regardless, the

process of identifying and naming our burdens is no small task in and of itself. If you're able to find the discipline and bravery to do it, I commend you.

And then, once we find those burdens and give them a name, we are (often) so deeply attached to them that we find that they have become a part of our very identity, making it nearly impossible to imagine who or what we might be without them. Who am I if not the insecure SLP? The stressed out Mom? The overworked student? What will be left for me to find of myself if I give up these characterizations and labels?

Friends, the process of letting go of what weighs us down is not easy. It can be scary to discover what is left when we strip them away. But, as an SLP who knows what it feels like to try to serve others when I haven't given myself what I need to "fly," I promise it is worth the work.

This week, I encourage you to find a quiet moment to identify what burdens you might be carrying, and what it would take to truly let them go. Maybe you'll even make the brave decision to step forward and break free from your past -- after all, you were born to fly.

Cheers,

Mattie

Courage to Ignite Change Challenge

"

Sometimes holding on does more damage than letting go.

Reflection Questions:

What are some of the biggest burdens or labels you are carrying around with you right now that are hindering you? List them below.

What has made these burdens so hard to "give up?" Why are you attached to them?

How do they/have they served you?

What do you risk if you don't let them go? What is at stake?

What is one burden or label you want to intentionally work to let go of?

What would the first step be?

Who could support you in this journey?

Significance Over Success

"
Success is about us. Significante is about others. John C. Maxwell

Hi Fresh SLP,

I am a bit of a dreamer. I can't help but look forward with anticipation at the future that lies ahead, hoping that the legacy I aspire to create will someday come to fruition. I imagine that many of you do the same thing as new or transitioning SLPs.

I've noticed, though, in these moments of dreaming, that it can be all too easy to become overly focused on being *successful*. Yet, I've found that aiming for success isn't always as useful as we may be conditioned to think it is.

For one, success is pretty tough to measure! It means different things to different people, and even our own definitions of success can change overtime as we grow. Ultimately, it's unlikely that any of us will wake up one day and all of a sudden feel convinced that we've *found* success -- it's just not the way it works. How, then, are we to measure our growth? Our impact? How will we know that we are making progress toward our dreams?

I think this quote from Oprah starts to give us our answer:

"*Don't worry about being successful. Work toward being significant, and the success will follow.*"

Work toward being significant. Hm! What an interesting way to reframe success as something that can actually be measured!

This quote got me thinking about all of the ways that we can each look for significance in our own lives and in our work as SLPs. In what ways do we make a difference? Where and how are we a part of improving people's lives in tangible, concrete ways? What changes are we creating in our workplaces and in our homes? Why does being an SLP even matter?

When we start digging into these questions that reveal the real significance of our work in the lives of others, we begin to uncover something much more important (and more tangible!) than success.

We start to see our legacy unfolding all around us in the here and now. In the **PRESENT.** We realize that we don't have to keep waiting and hoping to find *success* somewhere off in the distance. Rather, we have the opportunity to look carefully at the millions of little ways we are making an impact each and everyday, and know that we are, without a doubt, already leaving the legacy of our dreams -- if only we open our eyes and our hearts to see it.

Cheers,

Mattie

Courage to Ignite Change Challenge

> **"**
> *Success is fine, but success is fleeting. Significance is lasting.*
> *~ Beth Brooke*

Reflection Questions:

How have you defined success in your life?

_____

_____

_____

_____

How has that definition served and/or limited you?

_____

_____

_____

What weight/merit do you give to success? How important is it to you to be successful? Why?

In what ways has your life had significance/meaning?

In what ways have you found significance/meaning in your role as an SLP?

What do you want your legacy to be?

How can you start leaving that legacy today -- in big or small ways?

The Secret to Change

> **"**
> *If you are always trying to be normal, you will never know how amazing you can be. Maya Angelou*

Hi Fresh SLP,

Maybe it's just me, but there is something about the change of the seasons (hello Spring!) that gets me dreaming big. The fresh air and sunny days are so full of possibility, and they always seem to remind me that just as the seasons change, I too, am capable of real and meaningful change in my own life. What is "now" doesn't always have to be!

Socrates said that "The secret to change is to focus all of your energy not on fighting the old, but on building the new."

Friends, it can be SO easy to focus on what isn't working in our lives -- to dwell on our regrets and "misses" in ways that keep us stuck and feeling defeated. To wonder and worry about what was, or what could have been.

As new or transitioning SLPs in a competitive and complex profession, we can be incredibly hard on ourselves. I know, because I've been there. I know what it's like to engage in negative self-talk. I know what it's like to spend hours replaying a small mistake in my mind. I know how it feels to beat myself up over a decision I made.

And you know what? Being hard on myself has NEVER helped me create the changes I so desperately want to see in my life. It has never gotten me closer to my goal. It has never inspired me to do and be better. Rather, it has always been in the looking forward -- in the dreaming, in the imagining, in the building, in the manifesting -- that I am able to envision and create the changes I seek.

As we embark on the newness of spring, I challenge you to consider what new things you're committed to building in your life. What new skills and relationships do you want to invest in growing? What goals do you want to set and work toward? What do you want to do with your one beautiful life?

If you're willing to look ahead and be brave, I promise that the best is yet to come.

Cheers,

Mattie

Courage to Ignite Change Challenge

"
Whether you think you can, or think you can't - you're right.
~ Henry Ford

Reflection Questions:

Are you someone who tends to be hard on yourself and worry a lot about the past?

If so, where/how does this show up in your life?

How has this pattern of thinking impacted you?

Rather than reflecting on the past, what new things *(habits, relationships, etc.)* are you committed to building in your life?

What new skills and relationships do you want to invest in?

What goals do you want to set and work towards? Choose one of the new things you articulated above, and in the space below, come up with a concrete set of next steps required to make it happen!

Life Begins Where Your Comfort Zone Ends

"

Great things never come from comfort zones.

Hi Fresh SLP,

"Life begins at the end of your comfort zone." It's a phrase I've heard many times throughout the years, but it has taken me decades of experience to truly understand the gravity of its wisdom.

The unique thing about comfort zones is that it's hard to truly understand the size of your comfort zone *(and whether or not it needs to be expanded!)* unless you routinely -- and sometimes intentionally -- practice bumping up against the sides to test and explore its boundaries. As creatures of habit who prefer to stay comfortable and *safe*, I'll admit that this practice isn't one most of us routinely seek out -- myself included.

But what if we did? What if we did at least one thing every week *(or even every day?)* that scared us, just a little? What if we calmed the anxious voice in our heads that tells us to be afraid, unsure, or even insecure in new or unexpected situations? What if we embraced the opportunities life gives us to look for, find, and then **PUSH BACK** against our comfort zones in an effort to make them bigger?

If we all committed to doing this as new or transitioning SLPs, I have a feeling things might be different for us.

We might find that we are capable of doing *(and being)* more than we ever thought possible. We might find out who we truly are --- that person that others see and who we tend to discount when we look in the mirror. We might discover who we were actually **MEANT** to be in this life, if only we weren't afraid to be it. We might uncover the legacy that was destined for us.

What's more? We might realize that with boundary pushing comes some inevitable *failure*, and that failure *(as it turns out!)* actually isn't as scary as we thought. We might be more supportive and forgiving when those we work with (and those we love) take risks that don't pan out how they (or we) hoped they might. We might even be more forgiving and understanding of ourselves. Not just as SLPs, but as human beings.

As we move into a new week, my hope for you is that you are brave enough to find and push the boundaries of your comfort zone -- even just a bit. You might be surprised at the joy you find on the other side.

Cheers,

Mattie

Courage to Ignite Change Challenge

"
A comfort zone is a beautiful place, but nothing ever grows there.

Reflection Questions:

How comfortable are you pushing against your comfort zone in order to grow it?

_____

_____

_____

_____

_____

How often do you give yourself the chance to practice pushing against your comfort zone?

_____

_____

_____

How does it make you feel when you do it?

What's one area of your life where you want to challenge yourself to get outside of your comfort zone? Why?

Now or Never

Hi Fresh SLP,

Procrastination. It's a word that I have a complicated relationship with, and maybe you do as well. No one wants to admit they procrastinate. It isn't a trait that is positive or flattering, and putting off what needs to be done certainly doesn't help us reach our goals.

With that said, as a fresh SLP, there are *SO* many demands on your time. It can be easy to look at your goals and dreams and decide that there just isn't time to chase them today -- that they will still be there waiting for you tomorrow when your to-do list is shorter or your energy is greater.

But the thing is, we aren't guaranteed tomorrow! And what we put off today becomes less and less likely to manifest itself tomorrow, or the next day -- or ever.

As someone who knows what it's like to wait the extra day *(or week, or year!)* to chase their dreams, I encourage you to

Do it now. Because sometimes 'later' becomes never.

As we move into the spring season with renewed hope and energy, what have you been *putting off* until tomorrow? What goal, dream, or hope have you pushed back one too many times?

I challenge you to be courageous enough to give that dream or goal a second look with fresh eyes, and consider what it would *REALLY* take to commit to it in a way that would bring it to life.

I know you have what it takes to make **TODAY** the day that you start running toward that dream again. It is worth your every step, and so are you.

Cheers to moving forward,

Mattie

Courage to Ignite Change Challenge

"
Nothing in life is to be feared, it is only to be understood. Now is the time to understand more so that we may fear less. ~ Marie Curie

Reflection Questions:

What important things (tasks, dreams, goals) have you been putting off in your life?

_____

_____

_____

_____

Why are you putting them off?

_____

_____

_____

_____

What would it take to recommit to them?

What would be possible for you if you did?

Always Ask the Question

Hi Fresh SLP,

When I look back on my life, I realize that there were so many moments when I simply didn't have the answer. In the medical setting, with friends and family, and even within my own heart -- I find that I am so often faced with the profound and humbling challenge of simply not knowing what to do next.

As a new or transitioning SLP, that moment of "not knowing" can wash over you in an instant. It has a way of causing incredible insecurity, fear, and even panic. I know the feeling well, and I know how much more intense it feels when it happens in front of a patient.

The thing is, it is OK not to know! Becoming an SLP (and a good human being) is a process. It builds slowly and it takes time. Your expertise grows through dozens of small moments of learning -- learning from your professors, your colleagues, your patients, and yes -- even sometimes from yourself.

When it comes down to it, the best SLPs -- the ones who will truly leave their mark on the world -- know and understand that learning never ends. It continues after grad school, after you've landed your dream job, and after you've seen your 1,000th patient.

There is a proverb that says, "He who is afraid to ask is ashamed of learning."

I encourage you to remember that in those challenging moments of "not knowing," it is perfectly acceptable -- and encouraged! -- to simply ASK. Asking is how we learn. It is how we grow. It is how we change.

So the next time you find yourself without an answer? Own it! Lean with confidence into your curiosity. Proactively seek out an answer, and to come back to your patient with an update when one is needed.

Doing so doesn't make you less of an SLP -- it makes you a better one.

I've heard it said that the only fool in the room is the one who isn't brave enough to ask the question.

Cheers to being brave when bravery is required,

Mattie

Courage to Ignite Change Challenge

"
Don't dwell on what went wrong. Instead, focus on what to do next.
Spend your energies on moving forward finding the answer.
~ Denis Waitley

Reflection Questions:

In what areas of your life do you need to learn and grow?

_____

_____

_____

_____

_____

Who could you go to as a resource in those areas? What could you ask them?

_____

_____

_____

_____

What would it take for you to commit to seeking their counsel in this area?

What might be possible for you if you do?

You're Already Halfway There

> **"**
> *It always seems impossible until it is done.*

Hi Fresh SLP,

I was having a moment the other day where I let doubt creep in, and in a really big way. You know the kind of moment I mean -- where you second guess yourself at every turn, where you convince yourself you're not possibly good enough, capable enough, or strong enough to push through the challenges that stand before you. As a new SLP, I remember this feeling being so painfully familiar. At times, it was all-consuming.

If you've felt this way before - or if you feel this way today as you read this email - I encourage you to take some time to reflect on one of my favorite quotes by Theodore Roosevelt:

"If you believe you can, you're halfway there."

You see, what stops us from success - from reaching our potential and living out our legacy - is typically *NOT* those around us. It isn't usually a hard boss, or a critical friend, or even an unsupportive family member.

At the end of the day, the person often responsible for hindering our own success is us. We do it to ourselves!

We do it when we engage in negative self-talk. We do it when we pass on an opportunity because we aren't sure we can live up to the expectations. We do it when we over-analyze every move we make, searching for a way that we *must* have failed or messed up. We do it in a million small and big ways, and ultimately, it is these little attacks on our own hearts and souls that pile up and create the majority of our challenges.

So, if you feel like you're hitting roadblock after roadblock, consider if those barriers might be self-inflicted. Take an honest look at how you think about yourself, talk to yourself, and care for yourself. How do you feel when you look in the mirror? What do you really think of the person gazing back at you?

If you don't like what you see (or feel), you have the power to make a change! Just as you're responsible for setting one brick upon the next to build up the walls that ultimately limit your potential and hold you captive, so too are you powerful enough to knock the wall down entirely. To reframe the way you see yourself, and your place in the world.

And when you do? A whole new world of possibilities awaits you.

I know, because I've been there too -- so many times. And in that way, I write this message as much as a reminder for myself as a reminder for each of you. As Fresh SLPs, we are all in this together.

Cheers to believing in the power within you, and remembering that *you're already halfway there.*

Mattie

Courage to Ignite Change Challenge

"
I dwell in possibility. ~ Emily Dickinson

Reflection Questions:

When you look in the mirror, who/what do you see?

_____

_____

_____

_____

_____

In what ways might your thinking, mindsets, or patterns of behavior be holding you back?

_____

_____

_____

_____

Do you catch yourself engaging in negative thinking or negative self-talk?

If so, what positive mantras or phrases could you begin saying to yourself to reframe how you see yourself and your potential?

What might be possible for you if you became your own biggest champion?

Turning Adversity Into Advantage

> **"**
> *Every adversity, every failure, every heartache carries with it the seed of an equal or greater benefit.* ~ Napoleon Hill

Hi Fresh SLP,

I was thinking the other day about failure. I know, a fun topic, right?! But actually, I think it is one that deserves a lot more time and thought than we give it.

It's interesting how scary the word feels just to say it. Failure! There's something about it that feels so incredibly **FINAL**. Heavy. Permanent, even. But when I look back on my life, and really reflect on how my failures have impacted me, I notice a few things worth sharing.

First, failure isn't permanent! One of my favorite quotes:

"The comeback is always stronger than the setback."

Is a reminder of this fact. We will *ALL* fail and stumble as we do our best to bravely live out our legacy and purpose *(and if we don't, we probably aren't taking nearly enough risks!)*.

But what defines us is what happens next. What happens after the fall. Ultimately, we are defined not by our failures themselves, but by our ability to brush ourselves off, spend time in reflection as needed, and then begin again. Only then can we move forward with confidence, knowing that we've learned something new, and that we are now much better equipped for success.

Second, failure has a way of molding us into our best selves. They say that *iron sharpens irons*, and sometimes it is our very failures themselves that force us -- often with us kicking and screaming along the way -- to shed what isn't serving us, to let go where letting go is required, and to grow into a better, fuller, and more authentic version of ourselves. I know, without a doubt, that I am a better human *(and professional)* as as result of my failures, even -- and especially when -- they were hard to stomach.

Lastly, when you learn to fail fast and often, you realize that failure is as much a part of life as anything else. It plays a pivotal role in the shaping of our stories of self, in our relationships, and yes, even in our legacies as SLPs!

With these truths in mind, let's push ourselves to welcome the occasional moment of failure with open arms. To remember that the feeling of failure is fleeting, but the lessons learned, and the growth we enjoy as we emerge anew out of challenge, is with us forever.

Cheers to being brave in the face of failure, my friends. It's the only way to live.

Mattie

Courage to Ignite Change Challenge

> "
> *I can accept failure. Everyone fails at something. But I can't accept not trying. ~ Michael Jordan*

Reflection Questions:

What are your feelings/emotions surrounding failure?

_____

_____

_____

_____

_____

How comfortable are you failing?

_____

_____

_____

_____

In what areas of life have you experienced setbacks?

What would it take to turn those very setbacks into comebacks?

What might you need to let go of (mindsets, behaviors, beliefs about yourself) because they no longer serve you?

You Are Only Human

> **"**
> *Burnout is nature's way of telling you you've been going through*
> *the motions your sould has departed. ~ Sam Keen*

Hi Fresh SLP,

I read this quote the other day and it stopped me in my tracks:

> **"Burnout is what happens when you avoid being human for too long."**
> **~ Michael Gungor**

Read it again if you need to. Maybe three times to ensure it sticks.

Friends, it can be *SO* easy to jump on the hamster wheel of life -- especially as a new or transitioning SLP -- and just keep running. To look out around you and feel like everyone else is moving faster, doing more, or doing it better. To feel panic and anxiety set in as a result of comparison and ego, and to consequently push yourself harder -- just a little more, then a little more. Then a little more again.

Until you **BREAK**.

I've been there; more times than I'd like to admit. And if I had to guess? I bet you've found yourself there, too.

The thing is, our bodies aren't machines that can run forever. Our brains can only do our best thinking for so long without a break. Our hearts need connection with others. Peace. Alone time. Time for fun!

And ultimately? We can only give fully to others when we have given ourselves the rest and energy we need to ignite and unleash our passion. I hate to break it to you, Fresh SLPs, but we are only human.

If you're reading this and you feel exhausted and overwhelmed, first, know that you are not alone. Second, give yourselves a bit of grace! Our profession is one that is draining! A lot is asked of us and of our time. It is up to us to be connected enough with ourselves and our needs to sense when we are approaching burnout, and to jump off the hamster wheel well before we hit our limit. No one else can do it for us.

As you move through the rest of your week, I encourage you to check in with yourself and see if burnout might be creeping in. If so? Remember that it's OK to hit the pause button. To take a nap, take a run, or to a break. Whatever will fill you up to get you moving again. It makes you no less capable, deserving, or worthy.

After all, you're only human.

Cheers,

Mattie

Courage to Ignite Change Challenge

"
Take rest. A field that has rested gives a beautiful crop. ~ Ovid

Reflection Questions:

In what areas of your life do you find yourself nearing/past burnout?

_____

_____

_____

_____

_____

What impact does this reality have on you/other areas of your life?

_____

_____

_____

_____

What are three concrete changes you could make today *(or this week)* that would help refill your tank?

What support or resources do you need to make it happen?

What You Do Makes a Difference

"
What you do maked a difference, and you have to decide that kind of difference you want to make. ~ Jane Goodall

Hi Fresh SLP,

As a new or transitioning SLP, I know what it's like to wonder if you'll ever be "good enough" to make a true difference in the lives of your patients and their families through your career. We all go into this work with the desire to give to others, and it can feel hard, especially when we are still learning, to feel like we might never be knowledgeable enough, prepared enough, or experienced enough to make a true impact. We may wonder if we truly have what it takes to leave the legacy of our dreams.

When you feel this doubt creeping in *(and I promise we've all been there!)*, I encourage you to reflect back on one of my very favorite quotes from William James:

"Act as if what you do makes a difference. It does."

You see, the thing about *making a difference* is that it happens when we don't even realize it. It happens quietly, often in the tiny moments in life -- the ones you might miss if you aren't paying attention. In kind words, in a genuine smile, in showing another person care, concern, and empathy.

And the really good news? Even as a new SLP, you have the power to create an impact. You have the power to leave a mark on your peers, your supervisors, your patients, and their families. You can model the values you want to see reflected more broadly in the world. You can be the kind of professional -- and person -- that inspires others to be all that they can be.

YOU can make a difference. Not in ten years. Not when you have more experience. Not when you feel more confident or prepared. You can change the lives of others **RIGHT NOW.**

So, go out and do it! Don't wait to let your light shine! The world needs you now, more than ever before.

Cheers,

Mattie

Courage to Ignite Change Challenge

> ❝
> *You are not here to merely make a living. You are here to enable the world to live more amply, with greater vision, and with a finer spirit of hope and achievement. You are here to enrich the world. You impoverish yourself if you forget this errand. ~ Woodrow Wilson*

Reflection Questions:

What does *"making an impact"* **mean to you?**

_____

_____

_____

_____

_____

Who has made a significant impact on your life? How/why?

_____

_____

_____

_____

How can you create an impact and legacy of your own -- even in the small moments -- throughout your day?

The Power In Your "No"

> **"**
> *Give yourself the permission to say NO to anything that makes you unhappy and/or drains your energy.*

Hi Fresh SLP,

I don't know about you, but boy, am I a **YES** person.

If you're the same way, you'll know what I'm talking about. We tend to be quick to agree to things, quick to accommodate others' requests and demands, quick to take on new responsibilities and commitments. Yes. Yes. Yes. All. the. time.

Need me to take on a bit of your workload for you? Sure thing! Need help with a last minute project that I don't really have extra time for? No problem, I'll find a way to do it. Need me to pull some extra weight for the team? No big deal, I've got it.

And in some ways, this way of operating makes sense. As ambitious SLPs, it can be *SO* easy to want to stretch ourselves and say "yes" to all the things. With each new opportunity we take on comes a new chance for growth, and growth is generally a good thing.

But what about when we say one *yes* too many? Or five *yesses* too many? Or 10? The truth is:

"You can do anything, but not everything." -- David Allen

Are you capable of doing all of those things? Absolutely!

Should you try to do them all at once until you lose your mind? Absolutely not.

I know what burnout feels like, and it isn't fun. I know the stress of feeling overloaded with work and short on sleep. I know what it feels like to produce work that doesn't live up to my own expectations because I've simply taken on too much to do it all right.

And friends? This is no way to live. In the long run, it doesn't serve you, or anyone else -- even though it may feel like it does in that moment of the *yes*. There is no award in this life for the most *yesses* said, the most tasks accepted, the most to-do list items checked off. Ultimately, more isn't always more.

At the end of the day, your legacy is much more about the quality of your relationships and your work than it is about the quantity of it.

So the next time someone pushes you for a yes?

Pause for a moment. Really consider if you have the time, energy, capacity, and emotional reserves available to complete the task to your own standard.

If you aren't sure, tell them you'll think about it and get back to them. This is a strategy that isn't used enough, but that allows you to thoughtfully consider a request without feeling pressure to respond on the spot.

And if you know in your heart of hearts that you don't have the capacity to say *yes*, even if you *REALLY* wish you could, then for goodness sakes, get comfortable -- and I mean really comfortable -- with saying a polite no.

Is this easy to do? Nope, it is super hard.

Is it required of you as you grow into the SLP you're meant to me? Absolutely.

Cheers to finding the strength you need to commit to your *no*. I promise you it will make all the difference.

Mattie

Courage to Ignite Change Challenge

> "
> *It's only by saying NO that you can concentrate on the things that are really important. ~Steve Jobs*

Reflection Questions:

How do you feel saying *"no"* to others? What emotions / feelings come up for you?

Is it something you are comfortable doing or that you do often? Why/why not?

What stops you from saying *"no"* when you know you should?

When you say *"yes"* too often, what are the consequences? How does it play out in your life in real/concrete ways?

Where is one place in your life where you are saying "yes" too often?

What would it take to get brave enough to say *"no"* instead? Plan this out, and make it happen!

You Don't Have to Know It All

"

The more you know, the more you realise how much you don't know p the less you know, the more you think you know.
~David T. Freeman

Hi Fresh SLP,

I remember when I first started out as an SLP, I worried a lot about what I didn't know. It was so easy to look around at my colleagues with more experience and compare myself to them. I often doubted or second-guessed my own knowledge and skills, wondering if I really knew enough to fill my role. And to be honest? In some cases, I was probably right to do so. I was new! Many of you are new! It's OK to be in the process of learning. We don't start out *knowing it all*.

The good news? What will set you apart as a new or transitioning SLP isn't what's in your head -- it's what's in your heart.

Don Zimmer has a quote that I love:

"What you lack in talent can be made up for with desire, hustle and giving 110% of the time."

When you're a new SLP, what will set you apart probably isn't your perfect knowledge of all situations, and that's OK. You'll be able to rely on and learn from others with more experience as guides along the way. Soak in all you can from these mentors -- they are invaluable in countless ways.

But what *WILL* set you apart -- what will determine your ability to grow and be successful -- is your desire, your hustle, and your ability to give of yourself -- to your colleagues, and to your patients and their caregivers.

Go into work each day with an eagerness to learn. Ask good questions. Be curious! Work hard. Go the extra mile for a patient. Spend a few extra minutes mastering something new. Lend a helping hand to a colleague in need.

If you lead with these traits -- traits that require only an open and generous heart -- you'll easily learn the concrete skills and knowledge you need overtime, and you'll be loved and respected along the way.

Cheers to the journey,

Mattie

Courage to Ignite Change Challenge

"
Know your strengths and take advantage of them. ~ Greg Norman

Reflection Questions:

What special strengths or characteristics make you unique and set you apart from others in the field?

_____

_____

_____

_____

_____

_____

How can you leverage those strengths and let them shine more fully/more often?

_____

_____

_____

What do you hope people will remember about working with you?

You Don't Get Rainbows without Rain

> **"**
> *Everybody wants happiness, nobody wants pain, but you can't have a rainbow without a little rain. ~ Harihar Jena*

Hi Fresh SLP,

I don't know about you, but disappointment can land *REALLY* hard for us as SLPs. We tend to be over-achievers who are incredibly hard on ourselves (and, yet much more forgiving of others!), often doing all we can to ensure each and every aspect of our lives plays out exactly as we'd planned.

As much as we work to dot every *i* and cross every *t*, the truth is that there is no way to avoid the trials and stumbles of life. Things won't always go according to plan. Sometimes, disappointment and heartbreak are an unavoidable part of life.

The low grade you didn't expect, the CF you didn't land, the job that someone else got over you. These experiences can feel like gut-punches, taking the wind out of our sails and the confidence out of our hearts. I think we've all been there a time or two -- I know I have.

Dolly Parton once said:

"The way I see it, if you want the rainbow, you've gotta put up with the rain."

I think being an SLP is a lot like this. There are days where we feel the rain, and boy, does it pour-- **HARD**. Days where our patients struggle, where we get tough feedback from a supervisor, where we aren't sure we're cut out for this after all.

Sometimes we experience storm after storm, and we aren't sure when we'll see the sun again.

But friends -- we also enjoy **SO MANY RAINBOWS** as SLPs! Nailing a new skill, landing a dream CF, watching a patient recover with our help, being a beacon of hope to a caregiver who is tired and in need of a friend.

When I look back at my career as an SLP, I am humbled by all of the opportunities I've had to love people, to create an impact, and to use my skills in service of others. At the end of the day, our work is made up of so many tiny moments of grace, goodness, and light. There isn't much more I could wish for.

And I am thankful everyday for the rain --- because it gives me the rainbows.

Mattie

Courage to Ignite Change Challenge

"
Stay positive! Rainbows often appear when you least expect them
and need them most. ~ Jamie Worthington

Reflection Questions:

How do you handle disappointment? What emotions does it evoke in you?

_____

_____

_____

_____

What challenges have you faced in your journey thus far as an SLP? What rainstorms have you had to push through?

_____

_____

_____

_____

How have those challenges, disappointments and setbacks helped grow and shape you?

What unexpected rainbows emerged from the rain?

How might you challenge yourself to think differently about disappointment in the future?

Making the Invisible, Visible!

> **"**
> *Visualizing outcomes that you want can increase your confidence.*
> *"Seeing" yourself succeed helps you believe that*
> *it can - and will - happen.*

Hi Fresh SLP,

I've been told before that being able to bring a dream to reality has a lot to do with your ability to actually visualize it in your mind. To see it, feel it, and even experience it mentally in ways that give it power and momentum. This concept has always resonated with me, and it's one that I'm pondering a lot in challenging days.

With that in mind, Tony Robbins shares that:

"Setting goals is the first step in turning the invisible into the visible."

Have you set goals yet for the new year? If not, this is a gentle reminder that your ability to manifest your most precious dreams relies heavily on your commitment to setting bite-sized goals -- goals that you commit to in big and small ways, with consistency, each and every day.

Need help setting goals that get you to your destination? Take a stab at drafting a few goals in writing *(1-2 at most for the greatest success!)*, and check them against the **SMART** goals criteria below:

Ask yourself! Are they...

1. Specific

2. Measurable

3. Achievable

4. Relevant *(to your big dreams/aspirations)*

5. Time-bound

If not, make some adjustments to strengthen your chances of success, and start visualizing what it will be like to reach your dreams!

They are closer than you think.

Cheers,

Mattie

Courage to Ignite Change Challenge

"

Visualization is more important than knowledge. ~ Albert Einstein

Reflection Questions:

Use the space below to set 1-2 bite-sized goals, if you haven't already.

Now, check yourself: Do they each meet ALL of the SMART criteria outlined above? If not, edit them below to ensure you're set up for success!

The Power of Kindness

"

Kindness is giving hope to those who think they are all alone in this world. ~ Raktivist

Hi Fresh SLP,

We've finally did it! We are working our way through a pandemic and coming out the other end of what has been a long, hard, unprecedented few years as the pandemic swept our country and world. I reflect often on the many ways that people I know and love have suffered in profound ways these past few years -- loss of jobs, loss of loved ones, and ultimately loss of connection have taken their toll on all of us.

In a typical year, it would be tempting (and even wise!) to use this last week of the year to write an inspiring and bold post about setting -- and achieving! -- big goals in the new year. And if I did that, it wouldn't be all bad *(and I'll probably do it next week, don't worry)*.

But if I'm honest with myself -- if I'm quiet with my thoughts long enough to listen to them -- what is really on my heart during the last week of this incredibly hard year is not ambition. It isn't chasing your dreams. It isn't even goal setting.

What I'm thinking about most is the power of kindness. And specifically, what more I *(and we!)* can do to spread kindness like confetti as we head into this new year. A.A. Malee writes:

"Ah, Kindness. What a simple way to show others that there is love to be found in the world."

As SLPs in a *caring* profession, we have a unique opportunity, and responsibility, to lead with kindness in all we do. To assume the best, even when we have every reason not to. To extend a helping hand. To share a gentle smile, even on the days we are struggling ourselves.

I'm pretty sure that what the world needs most right now isn't more goals, more deadlines, or more ambitions. I think what we all need most right now is **LOVE**, and as far as I can tell, kindness is one the most concrete and universal ways we can show love -- in the big and small ways -- to those we encounter each day.

As we step into our lives and our careers, I hope we do all it with a little extra kindness in our hearts.

Cheers,

Mattie

Courage to Ignite Change Challenge

> **"**
> *Kindness is seeing the best in others when they cannot
> see it in themselves. ~ Raktivist*

Reflection Questions:

Who is someone who has had an impact on your life through their own kindness?

What did that kindness look like, and how did it impact you?

In what areas/spheres of your life could you spread more kindness?

Who are the people in your life who could benefit from extra kindness?

How can you show kindness in ways that are unique to you -- that utilize your strengths and interests?

Finding the Joy!

*Find joy in everything you choose to do. Every job, relationship,
home…It's your responsibility to love it, or change it.
~ Chuck Palahniuk*

Hi Fresh SLP,

As the end of the year draws nearer, I've been thinking a lot about what it takes to make our work sustainable in the long-term. There is no doubt that as an SLP, the days can be long and the challenges are great.

When I look back over my career as an SLP, what seems to keep me going -- even on the toughest days -- is being intentional enough to seek out little glimpses of joy that are all around me, even in the darkest moments.

Robert Louis Stevenson tells us to:

"Find out where joy resides, and give it a voice far beyond singing. For to miss the joy is to miss it all."

For to miss the joy is to miss it all. Wow. What profound wisdom.

This quote begs the question: What simple joys have you inadvertently been missing in recent days and weeks? Maybe it's a smile from a patient, a chance to pause and laugh with a coworker, or even the opportunity to slow down and enjoy a good book at the end of a long day.

As we move together into the final weeks of 2020, I challenge you to look with a grateful heart for the simple joys that are all around you. You just might be surprised to find more happiness waiting for you than you could have ever imagined!

Cheers,

Mattie

Courage to Ignite Change Challenge

> **"**
> *To find joy in work is to discover the fountain of you.* ~ *Pearl S. Buck*

Reflection Questions:

What are some of the simple joys in your life that you may be missing?

_____

_____

_____

_____

In what areas of your life do you want to commit to looking for more joy?

_____

_____

_____

What practices *(journals, meditations, etc.)* might you want to incorporate to help keep you accountable to focusing on looking for and celebrating joy?

Leaving Your Legacy

> **"**
> *If you are going to live, leave a legacy. Make a mark on the world
> that can't be erased. ~ Maya Angelou*

Hi Fresh SLP,

Have you ever thought about your legacy? About what your career as an SLP will do for and in the world?

Legacy is a funny thing. At first thought, we might be tempted to equate legacy with success. We often feel that in order to really leave our mark, we must get *straight A's* in grad school, get the best CF placement, and then land the perfect job with great pay and a prestigious title. *(Sounds pretty nice, right?!)*

If we view legacy in this restrictive way, we are bound to be held captive, like a hamster on a wheel, constantly searching, reaching, trying -- and never really feeling like we've done enough to be worthy of leaving a real impact.

At some point in my career, likely through the relationships I've formed with students and peers just like you, I came to understand that the legacy we leave as SLPs isn't about titles or prestige. It isn't about awards or acknowledgment *(though those things are nice).*

"What you leave behind is not what is engraved in stone monuments, but what is woven into the lives of others." - Pericles

Read that again if you need to. I know it hits home for me, and **HARD**.

As you look back on this year, how have you poured into others? How have you supported them? Loved them? Cared for them? As an SLP, we are honored to have these opportunities every single day.

The listening ear we lend to our patients, even when we're exhausted. The extra time we take to reassure a caregiver, even if we know their worry may not be warranted. The help we lend a colleague when we can see they are overwhelmed. The connection we forge with our clients, and the pain we feel when we leave them behind as second year students.

This, my friends, is our legacy as SLPs. And what a privilege it is to leave behind for the world.

Cheers to a career that allows us to give the best of ourselves.

Mattie

Courage to Ignite Change Challenge

> **"**
> *Carve your name on hearts, not tombstones. A legacy is etched into the minds of others and the stories they share about you. ~*
> *Shannon L. Alder*

Reflection Questions:

What legacy do you hope to leave behind? How do you want people to remember you?

_____

_____

_____

_____

_____

In what little ways are you intentionally working to build that legacy each day?

_____

_____

_____

Where could you be doing this more consistently or more fully?

Start Before You Are Ready

"

You can't plan for everything or you never get
started in the first place.
~Jim Butcher

Hi Fresh SLP,

It can be so tough not to overthink things in this job. If you're anything like me, you often find yourself filled with worry and self-doubt as you prepare to do something new, or as you grow your independence as a fresh SLP.

Will I say the right thing to my patient? Did I remember each step of the evaluation as I learned it? What if I forget something? What if I mess up?

The pressure to be perfect in our roles -- to know it all, do it all, to **BE** it all -- can feel crippling. In fact, sometimes that pressure can make it hard to start something new at all. It can keep us from stepping outside of our comfort zones, testing our limits, and learning about ourselves. In the end, that pressure to do it perfectly can actually keep us from moving forward.

As someone who often feels the need to over-think, over-worry, and over-plan (and boy is it exhausting!), the quote below has brought me so much bravery and peace during my years growing as an SLP:

"Success is to start before you are ready." - Marie Forleo

The truth is, we never quite feel ready to do the hard things in life. There will likely always be a voice inside of us that questions our readiness, our competence, our abilities. Ultimately, growing and maturing as professionals (and as people!) is about learning to quiet that voice, to give it a little less credit, and to be brave enough to take the next step forward, even when it feels really hard to do.

As we prepare for the holiday season and a new year ahead, I encourage you to take a good look at your life and see where you might need to simply start, even if you don't feel fully ready.

Even if you're unsure. Even if you are scared. You just might surprise yourself.

Cheers to the journey. It's worth every bump in the ride!

Mattie

Courage to Ignite Change Challenge

"
Thinking will not overcome fear but action will. ~ Clement Stone

Reflection Questions:

What have you been putting off in your life for fear that you aren't *"ready"*?

_____

_____

_____

_____

_____

What would it take to help you start *"before you're ready?"*

_____

_____

_____

_____

Create a plan below to tackle one goal/dream that you've been putting off.

Giving Up Yourself

"

"Why are you trying so hard to fit in, when you were born to stand out?" ~ Ian Wallace

Hi Fresh SLP,

It's funny how the pressure of life can get to you. It can make you feel like your life (or your career) has to look, sound, feel, BE a certain way. That there's one way to happiness and success -- and it's by following the road most traveled. That you *get there* by blending in, by meeting the expectations others have for you, by giving up little bits of yourself along the way.

What I've found to be true, however, is that the happiest and most successful people I know are completely, totally, and unapologetically **THEMSELVES.** They aren't afraid to march to their own drum - to stand out a bit from the crowd. And it is actually this very uniqueness that draws people to them. Like a moth to a flame, we know and instantly recognize authenticity. We crave it for ourselves, and when we see it in others, we are attracted to it.

This holiday season, as you encounter friends and family -- especially those who may have certain expectations of who or how you should be in the world -- remember that you were born to stand out; that the world needs exactly who **YOU** were made to be, and that success and happiness come with being fully and completely yourself. No apologies.

Cheers,

Mattie

Courage to Ignite Change Challenge

“

Authenticity: knowing who you are and
being brave enough to live it.

Reflection Questions:

In what areas of your life have you felt pressure to be a certain way? What has

that experience been like for you?

What would a more authentic version of yourself look like? What would you do?

Who would you be?

What is the biggest risk with pursuing your more authentic self? Is doing so worth the risk?

The Risk in Remaining Who We Are

> **"**
> *Too man of us are not living our dreams because we*
> *are living our fears.* ~ *Les Brown*

Hi Fresh SLP!

There is something about the shift in the weather -- the cooler days and the falling leaves -- that always gets me thinking about the concept of change. Of Evolution. Of Growth.

I don't know about you, but I've found that as humans, we tend to have a pretty complicated relationship with the idea of change -- especially when we apply it to ourselves. Sometimes we crave it; sometimes we dread it. Sometimes we don't even know we need it, when it's actually the very thing we need the most. Sometimes it happens quietly, slowly, almost invisibly, before we even recognize its presence in our lives.

While the experience comes with its fair share of complicated feelings, the ability to change, grow and evolve will prove pivotal to your success as an SLP. In an ever-changing field with diverse settings, contexts, and demands, we as SLPs will always be pushed to our edges, challenged in new ways, and forced to grow and change -- maybe in ways that feel uncomfortable or scary at first.

In those moments when you feel like you're on a runaway train that might just fly off the tracks,

I encourage you to reflect on this quote:

"We cannot become what we want by remaining who we are."
~ Max Depree

The interesting thing about change is that we actually **NEED** it in order to evolve into the person we desire to be. Regardless of how much we try to resist it, change will always find us -- gently nudging us closer to our destination. To our dreams. To our truest self.

My hope for you is that as you move forward in your career as an SLP, you find yourself able to embrace the changes you see in yourself with curiosity and confidence, that you lean boldly into your "growing edges," and that you ultimately come to appreciate and embrace the new, more full version of yourself that emerges on the other side.

I promise she will be a woman worth knowing.

Cheers to the you that you will become,

Mattie

Courage to Ignite Change Challenge

> **"**
> *Transformationally motivated people are the growing edge of a*
> *great continuity of souls reaching back to the very earliest times.* ~
> *Barbara Marx Hubbard*

Reflection Questions:

How do you feel about change? Do you generally embrace it, or avoid it? Why

do you think that is?

In what ways have you noticed yourself changing lately? How do you feel about

those changes?

What changes do you still hope to see in yourself? How might you help encourage them?

Boundaries

> **"**
> *Daring to set boundaries is about having the courage to love*
> *ourselves even when we risk disappointing others.* ~ Brene' Brown

Hi Fresh SLP,

Let's talk about boundaries. Having them, holding them, and following through on them. It's a concept that is pretty popular in the mental health space right now, and for good reason. But what is a boundary, exactly, and what does it have to do with my role as an SLP?

Boundaries are limits people set in order to create a healthy sense of personal *(or professional)* space. Boundaries can be physical or emotional in nature, and they help distinguish the desires, needs, and preferences of one person from another.

As an SLP, you are asked to give of yourself everyday, and doing so generously is a core part of your role. In fact, giving of yourself is very much a part of who you are, and a value you hold true. You give to your patients because you believe in them. You give to your company because that is required. You can often find yourself stuck between the two, and with the realities of COVID, it is harder than ever to establish and maintain healthy boundaries.

With that said, boundaries must exist in our work -- with patients, with caregivers, and with colleagues. As someone who is a fellow *giver*, I know this first hand how hard this can be in practice. I also know that the physical, mental and emotional toll of being regularly pushed past our boundaries is significant.

Here is one of my favorite quotes, again from Brene' Brown: When we fail to set boundaries and hold people accountable, we feel used and mistreated. This is why sometimes we attack who they are, which is far more hurtful than addressing a behavior or a choice.

So! What can you do as a new or transitioning SLP to set and maintain strong boundaries at work and in life?

1. Remember that you are allowed to say *"no."* You do not owe anyone your *"yes."*

2. Create space and time to figure out what you need, then **ASK** for it.

3. Act in accordance with your own values and beliefs, not those of others. Trying to be someone else is exhausting, hard, and ultimately, painful.

4. Take responsibility for your **OWN** happiness.

5. Do **NOT** take responsibility for the happiness of others.

Which one of these boundaries comes most easily to you? Which ones tend to be the most challenging?

Drop a comment on the post so we can continue to learn about each other's boundaries and **SUPPORT** one another on our journey.

Cheers,

Mattie

Courage to Ignite Change Challenge

"

I'm never more courageous than when I'm embracing imperfection,

embracing vulnerabilities, and setting boundaries with the people in

my life. ~ Brene' Brown

Reflection Questions:

What was your experience with boundaries like growing up?

Did your family set/adhere to healthy boundaries?

How did that play out?

What might those boundaries look/sound like?

Where might you need to say *"no"* more often?

Burnout

Hi Fresh SLP!

I was talking with a friend recently about the feeling of burnout I've been experiencing in my own life lately. You know the one I mean -- that feeling of exhaustion that you just can't shake. That never-ending racing in your heart. That looming feeling that there is always more to do. To say. To prove. To **BE**.

I think we've all been there. And yet, it can sometimes feel so hard to see out of the fog long enough to find your way again. To catch the breath you need. The break.

As someone who can be technically-challenged at times (*I'll admit it!*), I have to say I had a good chuckle when I encountered this quote about burnout the other day:

"Almost everything will work again if you unplug it for a few minutes -- including you." -- Anne Lemott

As it turns out, your TV really **WILL** come back to life if you just unplug it and plug it back in *(well, at least half the time)*, and I have to be believe that the same is true for us as humans.

If you're feeling stuck, as I have been, here are a few tips to battle burnout:

1) **Make Time for Yourself.** UNPLUG. Do what makes your heart sing (or just catch up on much-needed sleep, either way is cool). Seriously, this one is SO important. Don't skip it.

2) **Cultivate a Support Network.** Find *your people* -- the ones who will support you, love you, and hold you up. The ones who *get* your crazy. Hopefully, you can find some of those folks here. :)

3) **Set Limits.** Set them everywhere. In your personal life. In your professional life. EVERYWHERE. *(Got it?!)*

4) **Stay Grateful.** The truth is, you get more of what you focus on -- good, or bad. Wake up each day with a thankful heart (and maybe even write down a few things for which you are grateful), and you'll grow in peace and positivity.

5.) **Make a Change.** Even a small change to your routine can make a huge difference, and will help break the cycle of burnout.

So, here's to a kick-butt week of battling the burnout. I'm right there with you, my friends.

Cheers to the journey,

Mattie

Courage to Ignite Change Challenge

> **"**
> *The problem is not that women don't try. On the contrary, we're trying all the time, to do and be all the things everyone demands from us.* ~ Emily Nagoski

Reflection Questions:

In what ways have you experienced burnout in your own life?

_____

_____

_____

_____

_____

Which of the tips above feel most useful for you in combating burnout?

_____

_____

_____

_____

How might you incorporate them in your own life?

What do your next steps need to look like?

You Don't Need Fixing

"
Whenever you find yourself doubting how far you can go, just remember how far you have come. Remember everything you have faced, all the battles you have won, and the the fears you have overcome.

Hi Fresh SLP,

Have you ever doubted yourself? I mean in a big way -- the kind of feeling that makes you question your entire career path as an SLP? That makes you wonder if you're good enough? If you are **REALLY** cut out for this after all?

I've been there. I've doubted myself and my abilities more than I'd like to admit. I've felt the sting of failure in the medical setting when I wasn't sure how to effectively treat a patient, I've endured not getting the job I longed for, or the recognition and praise I thought I deserved.

To be honest, I think if you're in this field long enough, we are all destined to have these days. Being an SLP is not for the faint of heart.

When these tough days inevitably come and you are on the brink of losing confidence in yourself, I challenge you to remember this quote:

"When a flower doesn't bloom, you fix the environment in which it grows, not the flower." - Alexander Den Heijer

Friends, it may be your environment that needs changing --- not you! In fact, **YOU** are rarely (if ever) the problem. Whether you realize it or not, you have a unique set of talents and perspectives that the world needs; there is literally no one in the world who can do exactly what you can! You already have the raw materials within you to live a life you love -- you just have to plant yourself in the right spot.

Curious how your environment may be impacting your success? Ask yourself:

With whom am I spending time?

Are these people building me up, or tearing me down?

Am I in a work setting that plays to my natural strengths and passions?

Do I get to do what I love regularly?

Do I work with colleagues who support me fully?

Am I doing work that aligns to my values?

If you're brave enough to ask yourself these questions, you may just find that a change in your environment is all you need to bloom into the SLP (and human) you were born to be.

Worried about making lots of changes at once?

Don't be! Small changes can make a world of difference. Find a new colleague to spend your breaks with, ask to take on a few new responsibilities at work, propose small adjustments to your role that allow you to play to your strengths and show what you can do.

The world needs more of who you were made to be. Go out and find the soil that helps you bloom the brightest.

Cheers,

Mattie

Courage to Ignite Change Challenge

"

*You never know how capable you are until your passion
meets your determination.*

Reflection Questions:

In what areas of your life do you feel inspired to create change?

_____

_____

_____

_____

_____

How may your environment be contributing to your current situation?

_____

_____

_____

_____

In the space below, commit to one way you will work to change/shift your environment to better support the vision you have for yourself/your life.

Keeping Yourself Whole

Be passionate about yourself, do not sacrifice anything, and have fun.

Always remember to remain true and real to yourself.

Hi Fresh SLP,

I am a people pleaser -- and a pretty serious one, at that.

When I look back on my life, I guess I can see how I ended up here. I was raised to worry **A LOT** about how my actions, decisions, words -- my very **LIFE** -- would be received by other people.

Whether consciously or not, I learned to immediately read the room after sharing a big decision, opinion, or idea in order to evaluate how everyone else around me felt about it.

If I didn't get the reaction I wanted, I would quickly backpedal, qualify, or pivot to something else, even if it meant turning away from what I knew was right for me. Even if it meant letting go of a piece of who I was -- or who I wanted to be.

In short, I learned that it was more important to keep others happy than to be true to myself. It's a lesson that I continue to unlearn to this day, and will likely work on unlearning for the rest of my life.

Fresh SLPs, people around you often have their own desires, motivations, and needs for **YOUR** life. They may want you to live in a certain place, pursue a certain specialty, or take a specific job. While there is nothing wrong with considering the wisdom and input of others,

"You should not have to rip yourself into pieces to keep others whole."
~ Unknown

It is **NOT** your responsibility to make others happy, proud, or even satisfied. It is not your responsibility to follow in anyone else's path, fill anyone else's shoes, or make good on anyone else's dreams.

It **IS** your responsibility to live a life that is true to you **WHO** are -- a life that will make you proud at the end of your days -- regardless of how those around you may feel about it. This is a lesson that I learned the hard way, and many years later than I would have liked.

As you embark on a new week, I encourage you to be aware of places where you may be shying away from your own path in an attempt to follow someone else's. It may be easier for a time, but it is not easier for a lifetime. In the end, it is always easier *(and more joy-filled!)* to be totally, completely and authentically **YOU**.

Cheers to being strong enough to keep yourself whole,

Mattie

Courage to Ignite Change Challenge

If you stay true to yourself, you will never have regrets.

Reflection Questions:

Were you raised in a home that encouraged people-pleasing, even at the expense of being authentically you?

_____

_____

_____

_____

_____

In what areas of your life/around what people do you tend to people please? Why do you think that is?

_____

_____

_____

_____

What do you lose in the process? What are the consequences of doing this?

What would it take for you to make a change in this space?

Who could you confide in to help you stand up to others and be more fully you?

There is Room for ALL of us to Shine!

> **"**
> *Alone we can do so little; together we can do so much.*
> *~Hellen Keller*

Hi Fresh SLP,

I've been thinking a lot recently about competition within our industry. It seems that despite our best intentions, there is **SO** much pressure to *beat out* the SLP next to us. Whether it is pressure to be at the top of your grad school class, land the *best* CF placement, or get promoted into your dream role ahead of your colleagues, the sense that we must always be better than the person next to us seems to inevitably take hold.

When this feeling of panic and competitiveness takes over, threatening to steal my joy *(and it will, trust me!)*, I try to take a moment to remember this sweet, simple quote:

"The sky is full of stars, and there is room for ALL of them to shine."

Fresh SLPs, despite the pressures that are often placed on us in this industry, we simply don't **HAVE** to continue to be at such competition with one another. We don't **HAVE** to constantly fight and claw our way to the top, running endlessly on a hamster wheel to nowhere *(trust me, you'll never actually reach where you think you're going anyway -- you'll end up always wanting more, and nothing will ever feel like quite enough)*.

What if, instead of continuing to run the rat race to *the top*, we paused, pivoted, and challenged ourselves to look at things a bit differently?

What if, instead of competing with our peers and colleagues, we found ways to help them shine? To bring out the best in them? To lift them up?

What if they were just as committed to bringing out the best in you?

If we were all willing to look at ourselves and one another in this light, I think things might change for the SLP community. We might see more of us staying in the industry in the long run. We might build more meaningful friendships, and make memories characterized by **JOY** rather than stress. We might actually wake up each day and enjoy going to work.

After all, isn't that what you hoped for when you first decided to become an SLP? Isn't that the life you imagined for yourself?

SLPs, it isn't too late to chase that old dream. To bring joy, friendships, and fun back into our profession. We don't have to be each other's biggest competition. Let's try, instead, to be each other's biggest inspiration.

The future of the profession is ours -- let's ensure it lives up to our wildest dreams, and more.

Cheers to what's possible,

Mattie

Courage to Ignite Change Challenge

> **"**
> *It is literally true that you can succeed best and quickest by helping*
> *others to succeed. ~ Napoleon Hill*

Reflection Questions:

What is your relationship like with competition? Are you a competitive person?

If so/if not, how has that served or not served you in the past? What impact does it have on your life -- for the good, and for the bad?

In what ways can you build others up around you? Where do you have natural opportunities to do this?

Who is one person you want to commit to building up in the coming weeks?

The Joy is in the Giving

"

Happiness doesn't result from what we get, but from what we give.
~Ben Carson

Hi Fresh SLP,

Finding our purpose in life isn't always easy, and the path to becoming an SLP is not without its challenges. For many of us, deciding to become an SLP took an incredible amount of thought *(and maybe even some risk!)*, and while there are certainly challenging days in our profession, I am infinitely grateful that I was aware enough of my talents and passions to find my way into the SLP world.

As an SLP, I wake up each day feeling grateful beyond measure for the meaning and fulfillment that this work brings into my life, and to the lives of others. And I hope you do, too. Doing work that matters is a profound gift that I hope none of us take for granted.

That said, over the years, I've come to realize that while finding my gifts in life certainly feels rewarding, there is nothing more rewarding than sharing those gifts in service to others.

William Shakespeare summed up this sentiment well when he said:

> **"The meaning of life is to find your gift. The purpose of life is to give it away."**

Fresh SLPs, as we move into this next week, I challenge you to consider how you're *giving away* your gifts and talents in ways that help inform your legacy and define your impact.

In what ways are you allowing your unique talents, skills, and passions to be felt by your colleagues and clients?

_____

_____

In what ways are you highlighting your true gifts at work?

_____

_____

How are you giving of your most authentic self in ways that serve others?

_____

_____

In what ways are you using your gifts to help make the SLP profession better?

_____

_____

We've all been lucky to find our calling and passion as an SLP -- so many people will go through life never knowing what truly makes their heart sing.

But let's not forget that true joy is found not in the receiving, but in the giving.

Cheers,

Mattie

Courage to Ignite Change Challenge

"

We make a living by what we get. We make a life by what we give.
~ Winston Churchill

Reflection Questions:

How well do you feel that you know and understand your unique gifts? Do you need to spend more time uncovering them?

In what concrete ways are you using your gifts to serve others?

Where might there be additional opportunity to do so?

The Courage to Be Who You Really Are

> **"**
> *Everything you need is within you, the strength, courage, and*
> *confidence to change your life. You just need to look within yourself*
> *and find it. ~ Amanda Ray*

Hi Fresh SLP,

There was a point in my life when I thought I knew who I was. I was young, and pretty sure that I had it all figured out -- my values, priorities, strengths, vision for my life -- everything.

As I've grown and matured, it has become quite clear to me that in those early years, the woman who I thought I had become was really just a compilation of other people's definitions of me; my identity had somehow become defined by their priorities, their beliefs, their visions, and their expectations. I had somehow, unknowingly, absorbed them all into my consciousness, and spit them all back out into the world as *me*.

Looking back, my heart hurts for my younger self as I see -- much more clearly now -- how far from "me" that woman really was, and I didn't even know it.

Through hardship, transitions, experience and growth, we are challenged to unlearn what others have always told us about who we are. We are forced, sometimes painfully, to confront and acknowledge the true person inside of us -- the one who has been sitting quietly, patiently, waiting to be invited to step out into the light.

Learning who I really am, when I am brave enough to strip away all of the other *stuff* that has built up around my heart over time, has been one of the most transformative experiences of my life. It has also been one of the scariest.

E.E. Cummings once said:

"It takes courage to grow up and become who you really are."

It is clear to me, now more than ever before, that becoming who you really are requires not only courage, but also a willingness to take an enormous risk: you might just look in the mirror and not like who you see staring back at you. In short, becoming who you really are takes strength and bravery in great, bold measure.

This week, I challenge you to look within yourself with a gentle curiosity to see who might be waiting quietly inside. You might be surprised at the unfamiliar person who greets you, ready to have his/her moment in the sun.

Cheers to the bravery it takes to get to know that person, and to allow that person to show up in your life -- not just for your clients and colleagues, but for **YOU**.

Mattie

Courage to Ignite Change Challenge

"

Courage is resistance to fear, mastery of fear - not absence of fear.
~ Mark Twain

Reflection Questions:

What hopes, dreams, beliefs or aspirations do you hold quietly, without letting others see them?

What has kept you from expressing those parts of you in the past?

What do you risk by letting them out?

What might be true for you if you can muster the bravery you need to let them out?

Make Each Day Your Masterpiece

> **"**
> *Even with your flaws, you are still a masterpiece.*

Hi Fresh SLP,

As we say goodbye to the spontaneous days of summer and slip back into our familiar routines, it can be easy to switch our lives onto autopilot. To simply go through the motions of our day, checking off each task or obligation, only to have night fall and it occurs to us that we haven't really **LIVED** our day to the fullest. Maybe with the demands, pressures and stress we are under, we feel like we haven't really lived it at all.

Or worse yet, we let our anxiety, fear, and worry about tomorrow rob us of our joy today -- always looking ahead at what's next, and never enjoying the beauty of what is now. I've been there more times than I can count, and I'm sure many of you have, too.

Either way, friends, we are losing something. Something profound and precious that we can never, ever get back -- **TIME**.

John Wooden once said:

> ***"Make each day your masterpiece."***

I've thought a lot about those words recently, and how I am -- or am not -- truly painting each and every day with the brilliant, vibrant, reckless, messy, paint

strokes of emotion, experience, joy, laughter, bravery and **LOVE** that make life worth living.

I know now that life is meant to be **REALLY** experienced -- deep down to our bones -- in earth-shattering ways that change us forever. And we simply can't allow life to change us if we aren't showing up for it intentionally and fully.

SLPs, we only get one this *wild and precious* life. What will you do with it?

This week, as you head back into your fall routines, I encourage you to bring intentionality and vibrancy back into your days. Consider how you can be a gift to others, how you might take an unexpected risk, push yourself to learn something new, to take a new path, or to change something up.

Life is too short to be lived on autopilot. The joys that make up the best days of our lives are often right under our noses, if only we're willing to look up and grab them with both hands.

Cheers,

Mattie

Courage to Ignite Change Challenge

> "
> *The present moment is the only time over which we have dominion.*
> *~ Thich Nhat Hanh*

Reflection Questions:

What is your relationship like with time? How well do you use it? Why?

_____

_____

_____

_____

In what areas of your life do you find yourself on auto-pilot, checked out? Why do you think this is?

_____

_____

_____

_____

What feels missing from your life right now? Is it joy? Spontaneity? Adventure? Friendship?

Based on your response to question 3, commit to a set of actions that will help you bring that thing more fully into your life.

You Are Only One Choice Away

> **"**
> *Sometimes it's the smallest decisions that can change*
> *your life forever. ~ Keri Russell*

Hi Fresh SLP,

If you're anything like me, it can be easy to look at other people's lives and compare yours to theirs. Whether we know them in *real* life or only see their accounts on social media, we are likely all guilty of trying to measure our lives against the lives of others.

Why is everyone more successful than me? Why am I struggling to find my niche when others seem to have found theirs so easily? Why can't I figure out how to find fulfillment and joy in my career like *her*?

If we aren't careful, the comparisons can spin out of control. If you've been there, you know what I mean. This pattern of thinking *(and doubting!)* eventually robs us of our joy, and pulls us away from being our most authentic selves as we frantically try to *be like* those people who we *think* have it better than us.

And the thing is? They probably don't.

It's so very easy to paint a pretty, neat picture of your life and career for social media, or even when you casually run into an acquaintance who you rarely see. But at the end of the day, if you aren't in the trenches with people day in and day out, there is no way you can truly know their struggles -- struggles that you likely have, too. Struggles that we **ALL** have as humans who are trying to do our best as professionals in the world.

And what if they really **DO** have it that together, you ask? What if they really are living the life they've always dreamed of?

Well friends, you can too. At any moment, at any time, in any place...

"you are always one choice away from changing your life"
~Mac Anderson

The *you* of today does not have to be the *you* of tomorrow. Your destiny is not predetermined; you are responsible for shaping it each and every day, with every person you meet, every goal you tackle, every bond you form, every choice you make.

As you head into this new week, I encourage you to tune into the part of you that is yearning for growth and newness in your life -- that is looking at the lives of others from behind a computer screen or from across the street and wondering if your life can be just as special and remarkable as theirs.

It can. Go out and make the choices that get you there.

Cheers,

Mattie

Courage to Ignite Change Challenge

"

Live in the sunshine, swim in the sea, drink the wild air.
~ Ralph Waldo Emerson

Reflection Questions:

Where am I yearning for growth and newness in my life?

What would it take for me to achieve it?

What mindsets, actions, and choices would be required of me?

The Time is Now

"

Now is my time. Everything I've done up to this point is just a warm up. This is where it all begins. ~ Rick James

Hi Fresh SLP,

If you're anything like me, it can be easy to *put off* chasing your dreams. I know what it feels like to convince yourself that it just *isn't the right time*, or that there is no way you'd have a chance at success if you actually took the risk required to get started.

In fact, the amount of work we put into making a list of excuses **NOT** to go after our dreams is actually pretty impressive *(and a little sad, all at the same time)*.

"I need more experience first."

"I should wait until I have more money."

"I need a better network first."

"I'm not qualified."

"I'm just not "ready."

Fresh SLPs, I know what it feels like to have doubts stacked so high that you can barely see beyond them. I know what it feels like to be crushed under their weight.

It is paralyzing. It is painful. It is defeating.

But life has taught me that we will never feel quite ready to do the hardest, most important things in our lives. The decisions that require the most guts, the most bravery, the most risk, will **ALWAYS** feel scary -- like stepping off a cliff, not knowing if your safety harness will actually catch you.

But I think, if I'm being honest, those moments of complete terror -- those moments where I've pushed myself **FAR** beyond my comfort zone in the name of my dreams -- those are the moments that have come to define my life. They are seared into my memory like hot coal, always fresh and always full of emotion. They have shaped the person who I've become, and the person who I hope to be. They have shown me what I'm made of - that I am more brave, powerful, and capable than I ever imagined was possible.

This week, as you consider your next steps in your career and in your life, I encourage you to honestly evaluate what list of doubts or fears you have playing on repeat in your mind. (*And if you don't think you have them, try looking again, because we **ALL** have them. **ALL. OF. US.**)*

Once you've found them, (hello you pesky things!), bring them out into the open! Write them down if you need to -- throw them up on your walls on giant poster paper. Don't be afraid to stare them square in the face.

And then? Then decide if you are really going to let those fears win. Decide if you really want to choose a life of safety over one of adventure; a life of predictability over one of joy.

If you're like me, it will take every ounce of your bravery to muster up the courage to take the leap that your heart knows it is yearning for. But as Zig Zigler once said:

"What you get by achieving your goals is not as important as what you become by achieving your goals."

Don't wait. Please. The world needs who you were meant to be -- right now.

You are more ready than you know.

Cheers,

Mattie

Courage to Ignite Change Challenge

> **"**
> *Action is the universal language of success.*

Reflection Questions:

If you're being honest with yourself, what doubts/fears do you play *"on repeat"* to yourself?

_____

_____

_____

_____

_____

What does your negative self-talk sound like? List them below.

_____

_____

_____

_____

What phrases can you replace these with in order to take control of your life and create change?

What will your new self-talk sound like? Write it out below

You are the Artist of Your Own Life

> **"**
> *You are the artist of your existence, my dear. So color the canvas of your destiny and mold the shape of your reality. Never forget that above all else, your life is a masterpiece of your own creating.*
> *~ Becca Lee*

Hi Fresh SLP,

It is so strange to me that our lives can sometimes get **WAY** off course without us quite being aware that it is happening. One minute we are confident in the direction we're headed, and the next, we find that we have somehow ended up in a place *(job, relationship, city, etc.)* that we **NEVER** intended to be. Maybe it is even a place that we don't **WANT** to be.

That moment where you realize that you've somehow lost your way is like a gut punch to the stomach -- I know, because I've been there. Maybe you have, too.

So what happened? Why is it that we sometimes get *(super)* off course with our own lives? Where did we, quite unknowingly, make a wrong turn?

I heard a quote once that has always stuck with me:

> ***"You are the artist of your own life. Don't hand the paintbrush to anyone else."***

Now that I have a bit of life behind me, I can see in the rearview mirror that this quote actually holds one of the keys to staying on track toward our life's goals.

So often, we get off course because we have slowly, maybe even subconsciously, let other people's opinions, fears, desires, or expectations take the wheel in our own lives. At some point, we stopped listening to our inner voice and our own heart, and started allowing the voices and desires of others to drown us out. In short, we stopped living for ourselves. We gave the paintbrush of our life to someone else.

And look, I get it. This can happen so easily, and for SO many reasons. We may doubt that we really know what's best for us and therefore defer to others in times of struggle. We may have close family or friends with strong personalities and opinions that overshadow our own. We may even rely on others in financial or emotional ways, making us more susceptible to their influence.

But Fresh SLPs, at the end of the day, this one, sweet, precious life is **YOURS** and yours alone. At the end of your days, it is **YOU** who will have to look back on your life and determine if it was lived well, according to your own values and beliefs. At the end of your career, it will be **YOU** who cares most about the legacy and impact you have left for the next generation -- not anyone else.

You will, eventually, answer only to yourself. And what then? What will you see? Will you see a life authentically lived? Will you see a life that makes you proud?

As you move forward into this new week, I encourage you to pay special, tender attention to what your heart is calling you to do. Turn up the sound of your inner voice, and turn down the volume on the opinions that swirl around you.

If, in this moment of quiet, you find that you need to make some changes to realign your life -- to get it back on the track you intended for it all along-- then I wish you the courage and bravery to do what is required to make that happen.

This isn't a dress rehearsal, my friends. This is it. You only get one shot at this life. Pick up the paintbrush and make it **YOURS** -- and yours alone.

Cheers,

Mattie

Courage to Ignite Change Challenge

"
Everything is figureoutable. ~ Marie Forleo

Reflection Questions:

In what areas of your life have you *"given away"* the paintbrush, and to whom?

Why do you suspect this has happened?

Setting aside the wishes/influences of others, what do **YOU** desire for your life? What legacy do you want to leave?

What is one thing you can do this week to begin to take back the paintbrush -- and take back your life?

Do What Makes You Come Alive!

> "
> *There is no greater gift you can give or receive than to honor your calling. It's why you were born. And you you become truly alive.*

Hi Fresh SLP,

Whether you are a new or seasoned SLP, I think we all have days where we wake up and go about our life on autopilot. These days are often lived in survival mode -- simply going through the motions of our schedules and checking off our to-do lists, all the while feeling entirely disconnected from our passion and purpose. It is a state of being that has become all too familiar to many of us.

I hate to admit how often these days happen for me, in part because when I was deciding what career to pursue many years ago, it was my very passion for this work that inspired me to become an SLP! I so badly wanted to serve, to teach, to support, to inspire. I wanted to play a small role in helping my patients transform and improve their lives, despite the odds that may be stacked against them. I wanted to know that the work I did each day mattered -- not just to an organization's bottom line, but to individual hearts and lives.

When I was discerning my career path, I remember coming across this quote:

Don't ask yourself what the world needs. Ask yourself, "What makes me come alive?"... because what the world needs is more people who have come alive. - H Thurman

Fresh SLPs, even on the hardest days -- the days where our energy and inspiration feel lacking -- we must not lose sight of **WHY** we became SLPs in the first place. We chose this work because it truly does make us come **ALIVE**. It reminds us of what it means to be human, to be connected to others, to know that what we do **MATTERS** in this crazy world. And it does. Infinitely.

So this week, when you feel a slump coming on -- when you're tempted to switch into autopilot -- I challenge you to return to your **WHY**. I challenge you to return to your passion. I challenge you to focus on what it is about being an SLP that makes you come alive, and lean into that with all of your might.

Maybe you have to write out your *why* and stick it on your computer monitor so that you can read it each morning. Maybe you have to start and end your day with gratitude. Maybe you have to spend a little extra time with a patient who brings you joy.

Whatever you need to do to find your passion again -- do it. You owe it to your patients, to the profession, and most importantly -- to yourself.

As SLPS, we are lucky that there is so much joy and meaning to be found in our everyday -- don't let it pass you by.

Cheers,

Mattie

Courage to Ignite Change Challenge

> **"**
> *Life is not made bearable by circumstances, but only by lack of meaning and purpose. ~ Viktor Frankl*

Reflection Questions:

What is your *"why?"*

Where do you find your passion? Your energy?

What makes you come alive?

How can you better center your *"why"* in your life? Can you display it? Repeat it? Share it? Create a plan below to bring your *"why"* back into focus.

A Worthy Pursuit

"

Some people dream of success, while other people get up every morning and make it happen. ~ Wayne Huizenga

Hi Fresh SLP,

When I was just starting out in my career, I recall feeling like there were never enough hours in the day to learn all I wanted to know about our profession. I was amazed at the depth of knowledge and skill required to do our work well, and I committed myself to learning all I possibly could in school and in my placements on behalf of my future patients. It was a worthy pursuit, and not one I regret. I'm sure it helped form me into the capable technician and professional I am today.

But looking back, I think there was something else I could have been seeking out more intentionally in those early years -- something that seemed to evade me until later in my career. It wasn't a specific skill, evaluation or piece of knowledge. It wasn't even something I could find in a textbook.

It was wisdom.

Years ago, I heard a quote about wisdom that has stuck with me to this day:

"Never mistake knowledge for wisdom. One helps you make a living. The other helps you make a life." ~Sandra Carey

Fresh SLPs, hear this. The pursuit of gaining knowledge is a worthy one! It is important. It is critical, in fact, to ensure you are equipped to do your job well and keep your patients safe. You have a moral and ethical obligation to gain the knowledge required of you to execute your role effectively.

But, knowledge isn't all you need to be a great SLP. It isn't the thing that will ultimately help you find success, fulfillment, peace or joy in this role -- or in this life, for that matter.

For that, you'll need wisdom. You'll need good judgement. You'll need something beyond what is found in textbooks. So how do you get it, then? How do you become wise?

First, look beyond the textbooks and into the world to help shape and grow you. Push yourself to engage in new experiences, get to know new people, and take on new risks. Remember that life itself -- experience itself -- is often your greatest teacher. Never underestimate its power, and always find ways to show up for your life in new and scary ways. I promise you'll be glad you did.

Next, seek out mentors who you can teach you and provide you with counsel. There is no substitute for the sound advice of someone who cares about you, who knows you, and who has walked in your shoes. If you don't have role models in your life who you can ask to be your mentors (yes, you should formally ask!), then seeking those people out should be your top priority.

Lastly, remember that in so many ways, wisdom comes from within. In your hurry to go out and experience the world, read your textbooks, and learn from your mentors -- don't forget to find time (on a regular basis) to quiet everything around you so that you can tune into the voice within you. Don't forget that your heart's deepest desires and dreams can often hold the greatest wisdom of all.

Cheers to the pursuit of wisdom. Few things are more worthwhile.

Mattie

Courage to Ignite Change Challenge

"
To attain knowledge, add things every day. To attain wisdom,
remove things every day ~ Lao Tso

Reflection Questions:

In what ways are you pursuing true wisdom, not just knowledge?

_____

_____

_____

_____

_____

Who could help mentor and guide you in pursuit of wisdom?

_____

_____

_____

_____

_____

What new life experiences could help you grow in wisdom?

What can you learn from yourself? What does your heart tell you?

Life Isn't Always What It Seems

"

Perspective is everything when you are experiencing the challenges of life. ~ Joni Eareckson Tada

Hi Fresh SLP,

Recently, I had one of those days where it felt like nothing would go right. I overslept and rushed out the door for work. I forgot to bake a dessert for the staff potluck at work (whoops), and when I got home -- starving and exhausted -- I discovered, much to my dismay, that I had forgotten to turn on my crockpot that morning as I ran out the door. After feeling sorry for myself on the couch for awhile, I dragged myself out to get fast food, and went to bed feeling drained, frustrated and annoyed.

It was what most would call a *bad day*.

The next morning, a colleague stopped me in the hall to chat. Before we parted ways to see our next patients, she mentioned how grateful she was to work alongside me, and what a *rockstar* I was in her eyes. She said she had noticed how I had brought a smile to my elderly patient's face yesterday during an evaluation (despite running through the door 5 minutes prior), and how I had bonded and laughed with one of our fellows while I helped her tackle some of her grad school work over lunch. She saw me humming happily to myself while I filled out some paperwork and sipped my morning coffee. She saw me hug a friend who stopped by my office over lunch to say hello.

stopped in my tracks for a moment as I watched her walk away.

Wait a minute.

Didn't I have a *really bad* day yesterday? Didn't *everything* seem to go wrong? Didn't I go to bed upset and defeated?

At that moment, I remembered a quote that I had heard when I was very young. Its meaning was all of a sudden more poignant than it had ever been before.

"What we see depends mainly on what we look for." - John Lubbock

Fresh SLPs, so much of life is about perspective. What you get out of your day -- the way you experience it, see it, talk about it, and reflect on it -- is in so many ways dependent upon **YOUR CHOICES**.

What you choose to focus on. What you choose to *center* in your thoughts. What you give the most space in your mind and in your heart.

It took me too many years to learn this simple but profound lesson, and I mourn for all the little joys, happy moments, smiles, and connections I failed to notice because I simply wasn't looking for them. Because I was too busy focusing on the negative, the frustrations, the annoyances.

I will never get those moments back. What I can do is work hard, everyday -- in big and small ways -- to shift my focus to what is good.

To what is pure.

To what is lovely.

To reframe each moment in the positive.

To recount the story of my life in a way that makes me proud.

To give credit where it is deserved.

As you move into this new week, my wish for you is that you can work to do the same. Your perspective won't change instantly. But with disciplined thinking, practice, and self-reflection, you can truly change the way you experience your own life. With enough work, a *bad day* you lived 10 years ago could feel like one of your better days if you re-lived it again tomorrow, all with a simple but intentional shift in your perspective.

It is possible; I promise. Go out and make it so.

Life is too short for anything else.

Cheers,

Mattie

Courage to Ignite Change Challenge

***

"

Your perspective will either become your prison or your passport.
~ Steven Furtich

Reflection Questions:

What do you tend to *"look for"* or see most often throughout your day?

Why do you think this is?

Thinking back to your day today, what are 3 positive, lovely, pure things that you experienced?

How can you more regularly build gratitude and a focus on positivity into your days?

The Beauty In the Climb

"
The oak fought the wind and was broken, the willow bent when it must and survived. ~ Robert Jordan

Hi Fresh SLP,

If you're anything like me, you probably have a plan mapped out for your career. In one way or another, you likely have a vision in your mind (or maybe even on paper!) of what you hope to achieve. And that's a good thing! Visioning and goal setting is an effective and worthy practice -- never stop doing it. It will serve you well in more ways than you can imagine now.

That said, I've learned through the years that the road to reaching your goals isn't always as linear or smooth as we hope. There are almost always bumps and hurdles along the way. Experiences that fall short of our expectations. People that hurt us. Disappointments. Crippling doubts.

But Fresh SLPs, please remember this: no good thing is easy. In fact, most good things in life are hard! Despite your tireless efforts and genuine intentions, it is a fact of life that sometimes you will have to watch what you desperately hoped and wished for slip right through your fingertips.

The *perfect* CF.

The *perfect* supervisor.

The *perfect* setting.

Sometimes, Fresh SLPs, it turns out that what we hoped was going to be ours, isn't really meant for us after all. Sometimes all of our planning, our plotting, and our wishing leads us to a dead-end. Maybe even to a heartbreak.

But the good news?

There is always another path waiting just around the corner, spread out toward the horizon like open arms, ready to welcome us into what IS meant to be, if only we can muster up the courage to keep walking. To keep seeking. To keep looking. To keep putting one foot in front of the other with humility and hope.

You may be forced to take unexpected routes to get to your career goals. You may have to double back, or even scrap your plan all together and come up with a new way to get to your destination.

But when you do? When you **FINALLY** reach the top?

It will be worth every moment of heartache. Every disappointment. Every letdown. Because ultimately,

"The best view comes after the hardest climb."

Fresh SLPs, the view from your new *(and likely unexpected!)* mountaintop will take your breath away. I promise. It will be better than anything you had imagined for yourself, because it will be what was truly meant for you all along. Even when you didn't know it. Even when you were struggling desperately to see how the journey would end.

This week, as we push toward the break that comes with the holiday season, I challenge you to get comfortable with the climb. To settle into the discomforts that come with changes in course, with barriers in the road. With learning who you are meant to be -- as an SLP, and as a human being.

It isn't always easy. But I promise you, it is always worth it.

Cheers to the climb,

Mattie

Courage to Ignite Change Challenge

_____

"
Persistence and resilience only come from having been given the chance to work through difficult problems. ~ Gever Tulley

Reflection Questions:

In what ways are you *"climbing"* through life right now?

_____

_____

_____

_____

_____

What challenges/setbacks have you experienced lately?

_____

_____

_____

_____

_____

How have you reacted to discomforts/challenges along your journey?

What is one goal you can set for yourself to better handle challenges in the future?

Are Your Habits Serving You?

> "
> *Your habits will determine your future.* ~ Jack Canfield

Hi Fresh SLP,

Are you one of those people who has a *morning routine*? You know, the ones you read about in all the self-help/ personal growth articles. They talk about waking up *30 minutes before your day really starts*, and doing some set routine that helps set a positive, healthy tone for the day -- reading, exercise, meditation, whatever.

Well, I want to be a morning routine person. I really do. I can so easily see how powerfully that kind *sacred* time could impact my day, my mindset and my emotions in profound ways, and I've been super motivated to make it happen.

And yet, it hasn't happened. For years now.

Well, let me rephrase that. It has happened a few times. Inconsistently. Maybe for three or four days straight, then it stops. I may pick it up again when I get renewed energy in the idea, but then drop it just as quickly as I have in the past.

I can't help but think: why is this happening?

This is something I'm **CAPABLE** of doing. I've certainly done much harder things in my lifetime. I know **HOW** to do it. I have all the **RESOURCES** I need to do it.

I **WANT** to do it -- badly!

So what's going on here?

The answer lies in a quote from Jim Ryun that is applicable far beyond morning routines, and into all areas of our lives as SLPs:

"Motivation is what gets you started. Habit is what keeps you going."

Looking back, I struggled with establishing a morning routine not because I didn't see the value in doing it *(my motivation was there, trust me!)*, but because I hadn't taken the time to create, schedule, and commit to a concrete plan *(a set of habits!)* for how I was actually going to make this happen.

All the time.

Without fail.

Even when life got in the way.

I understand now that I would have been more successful if I had prepared for my morning routine the evening before by setting my workout clothes and daily journal next to my bed. I should have set an alarm each and every evening to remind me to go to sleep at a reasonable hour so that I could actually wake up when my "morning routine" alarm sounded. I should have called a friend and told them about the plan so that we could do it together for some accountability.

In short, I should have created actionable habits that would have set me up for success.

Fresh SLPs, as we inch toward the end of this year and begin to look ahead to the New Year, I encourage you to take a hard, honest look at your habits.

Do your habits align with your values?

Do they support your goals?

Do they help you bring your dreams to life?

Are they actionable?

Are they consistent?

If not -- if you're dreaming and wishing without giving yourself the structure you need to be successful -- then as hard as this may be to hear, you are doing yourself a massive disservice. Whether it is studying for grad school exams, learning something new in a CF, or working toward a goal in your career, I challenge you to remember (and act on the fact!) that it isn't your motivation that will get you there -- it is your habits.

Habits are hard to create. I know. Some research has suggested that it takes 33 days straight of doing something **DAILY** to make it a habit. **33 DAYS**!

But I promise, the effort invested in staying consistent and disciplined will pay off ten-fold when you get to watch your dreams begin to come to life in front of you. When you all of a sudden become the "morning routine" person -- or the SLP -- that you've always wanted to be.

I've been there, and I know it is possible for you, too.

Cheers,

Mattie

Courage to Ignite Change Challenge

> **"**
> *You will never change your life until you change something you do daily. The secret of your success is found in your daily routine.*
> *~John C. Maxwell*

Reflection Questions:

What new habits have you been wanting to create in your life? Why?

_____

_____

_____

_____

_____

How can you make those habits more concrete and actionable?

_____

_____

_____

_____

What bite-sized goals can you set for yourself that you can track and follow up on regularly?

How can you create accountability for yourself?

Finding the JOY

Hi Fresh SLP,

If you're anything like me, some days as an SLP can feel like a struggle. Truly. Some days are just incredibly hard.

The moments when you make a misstep treating a patient. The days when you just can't seem to provide the right support for a worried family. The times when you feel completely and totally inadequate in your role.

Trust me, I've been there. We **ALL** have. If there is anything that unites us as SLPs, it is the fact that this work is hard no matter what your setting, and even more than that, we can all be so very hard on ourselves.

We are often our own biggest critics, most skeptical juries and toughest judges. We can play out entire scenes in our head where we put ourselves down, question our capabilities, and second-guess our decision to pursue such a challenging field, wondering if we really have what it takes.

But friends, this isn't the life we were meant to live. We didn't choose a "helping" profession so that we could help others only to beat ourselves up! We chose it because it brings us fulfillment. It brings us happiness. It brings us **JOY**.

Walt Whitman said:

"Do anything, but let it produce joy."

So Fresh SLPs, I ask you: In what ways are you using your role to produce joy?

Joy for you? Joy for your patients? Joy for your colleagues?

In the big moments, and in the small?

How can you begin to reframe this work as not just challenging, but even more than that, joy-filled?

Because at the end of the day, you will only be as effective as you are happy in this work. You can't possibly be your best self for your patients if you are overcome by crippling negativity, doubt, and self-criticism.

Your patients deserve to have you fully present, fully alive, and fully **JOYFUL**.

And you know what? You deserve that, too. More than you know.

Cheers to finding the joy,

Mattie

Courage to Ignite Change Challenge

"
Find a place inside where there's joy, and the joy will burn out the pain. ~ *Joseph Campbell*

Reflection Questions:

In what areas of your life do you currently find joy?

_____

_____

_____

_____

How might you seek and find more joy in your current role?

_____

_____

_____

_____

How might things change for you if you start focusing more on the joy? What outcomes do you hope for?

You Are More Than Enough

> **"**
> *You are enough. You were born being enough. Nothing you say or do will ever add to or subtract from who you are.~ Jenny Layton*

Hi Fresh SLP,

I just recently returned from the ASHA Convention, where I was absolutely blown away by the people I met and the connections I made. I left feeling energized about the future, hopeful about what's next for our profession, and more passionate than ever about pouring my heart and soul into Fresh SLP.

And if I'm being totally honest, at the same time, there were moments where I doubted if I was really worthy of being there -- if I could really *stack up* against the other leaders around the room who all seemed to be oozing with confidence (and lots of really cool swag!).

Questions started swirling in my mind the moment I walked into the convention space:

"Is my booth going to be appealing enough?"

"Did I bring the right freebies?"

"Will the products and programs I'm featuring paint a clear enough picture of the beautiful heart and soul of this community?"

"Have I done enough to prepare for this weekend?"

After taking a breath and centering myself for a moment, I was able to stop myself from spiraling into the full-on chaos and self-loathing that comes from comparison. I was able to remind myself that I was worthy of being there -- that I was enough. And more than that, as I let the positive energy of the room overtake me, I was overcome with another familiar feeling.

It wasn't worry.

It wasn't self-doubt.

It wasn't insecurity.

No.... It was gratitude.

Gratitude for having the chance to be here when many others could not. Gratitude for having the privilege to grow the Fresh SLP into the vibrant community it is today -- a community I couldn't have dreamed of a decade ago. Gratitude for the ways in which this community comes together to support and nurture one another. Gratitude for getting to do work that feeds my soul.

And just like that,

"Gratitude turned what I had into enough."-Aesop

I was no longer worrying if my swag was cool enough, if I was young enough, or if my booth was eye-catching enough. Instead, I was totally at peace -- filled to the brim with an authentic and overflowing gratitude that had turned what I had -- and who I am -- into enough.

As we continue in this holiday season, I wish the same for you. I wish you the same sweet moments of joy where you are absolutely overwhelmed with gratitude for the life you've built for yourself, even if it is far from perfect.

And even more than that, I wish you the confidence to know that you are always -- in every single little moment and in every single little way -- so much more than enough.

Cheers,

Mattie

Courage to Ignite Change Challenge

"

Acknowledging the good that you already havein your life is the foundation for all abundance. ~ Eckart Tolle

Reflection Questions:

In what areas of your life do you find yourself comparing yourself or your life to others? Why?

How does comparison impact your life?

In what areas of your life are there opportunities to focus more on gratitude?

Don't Look Back

> **"**
> *The past is like an anchor…you need to let go of who you were, to become who you'll be.*

Hi Fresh SLP,

As the year inches toward its close, I can't help but begin to reflect back on how it has measured up against the goals I set for myself this time last year. If you've been around since then, you might remember my challenge to you to commit your goals for the new year to paper, and put it on display to help focus your efforts.

It took me longer than I'd like to admit to track down that pesky little list of my own *(so much for keeping it visible, huh?)*, and when I finally did find it among a stack of *important papers* on my desk, I have to be honest with you -- my heart sank, just a little.

Did I accomplish some of what I wanted to accomplish this year?

Certainly! More than anything else, I am deeply proud of how the Fresh SLP community has grown and matured this year, and for the clarity I've gained -- alongside all of you! -- about where it needs to go in the future to continue to meet your needs. This year has been exactly what we all needed in that sense, and I'm grateful for the chance to continue the journey with you into 2022.

And yet? Lots of goals went unaccomplished. Lots.

As I scan the list, I feel a tinge of guilt everytime I read something that I didn't quite *get to*. The new morning routine, the boundaries I planned to set around certain personal relationships, the mindset work that I hoped to *master* this year, the hobbies I intended to take up for some more *me* time.

I was starting to feel sorry for myself in a major way when I remembered a quote that I heard for the first time decades ago -- one that has stuck with me until this day.

"Don't look back - you're not going that way."

Fresh SLPs, it is so easy to be hard on ourselves - especially in this profession. To be our own biggest critics. To expect more of ourselves than we would ever expect of others. I know, because I've been doing it for years. (Please tell me I'm not the only one?!)

And yet, life can't be lived looking in the rearview mirror. Lamenting over my unmet goals all day in my office doesn't serve me, my spirit, or my motivation. Ultimately, the most loving thing I can do for myself, and the thing that will actually help inspire me to try again next year, is to acknowledge what didn't happen -- and let it go.

And at that moment, sitting there in my office with the dusty old list in my hand, I did just that. I decided to release the disappointment and the pain that comes with unmet expectations. I put a lid on the negative self-talk. I stopped re-playing my mistakes and missteps throughout the year on a loop in my mind.

And instead? I focused on the wins! I dove headfirst into a space of gratitude, thinking fondly about all those kick-ass people who had helped me accomplish the goals that I met (or exceeded!) on that list. And with that simple shift in focus, I went from feeling defeated to feeling empowered.

And you know what? I'm ready to make that list again. To pin it up on my office wall, and work like heck to keep it out of the *important* stack of papers on my desk.

But what if it does end up there?

What if I still fall short when I read it next December?

Well, then I'll be human. And I'll try with all of my might to give myself the grace and forgiveness that I would so easily -- and without hesitation -- extend to others. I will gently remind myself that perfection is not the end game. It isn't the goal. And isn't what brings happiness in this life.

Failure is a part of life. Love yourself through it, and you'll be that much more likely to nail it the next time.

Cheers to starting anew.

Mattie

Courage to Ignite Change Challenge

"
*Look forward in your life and regrets are no more. ~ Sandeep
Ravidutt Sharma*

Reflection Questions:

How do you feel about the goals you achieved *(or didn't achieve)* this year?

_____

_____

_____

_____

Where do you find yourself being your own biggest critic?

_____

_____

_____

_____

How do you want to think about/approach goal setting for next year?

How do you hope you handle/react to any potential shortcomings you may notice this time next year when evaluating your progress to goals?

A Note From The Author

I would love to hear from you and how this book, **Lessons on Becoming: 52 Weekly Inspirations & Reflections on How to Become the SLP You Were Meant to Be** has made a difference in your life and career! Please share your stories, insights, challenges, and reflections with me. I'd love to hear from you! - Mattie Murrey Tegels

Contact Mattie On Social Media

IG: FreshSLP   IG: BadassSLP

FB: Fresh SLP | Facebook

Email: Mattie@freshslp.com

Website: www.freshslp.com | www.badassslp.com

Linked In: Martha (Mattie) Murrey-Tegels | LinkedIn

Podcast: www.freshslp.com/podcast

Acknowledgements

This book has been a labor of love and learning and reflection and hopefully a start to a legacy that I leave for future SLPs.

First, I would like to thank my colleague, Dr. Janet Tilstra, who planted the seed for this book. She has a been a friend and a source of inspiration for some of these reflections.

I'd like to thank Kate Peabody, a life coach that taught me to dream and how to make those dreams actually come true through vision boarding, goal setting, and road mapping. I would not have believed, at the start of our work together, all that I would accomplish to this day

I'd also like to thank Layne Pratt, my writing partner for this book. We share the same voice and you are indeed a gifted writer. I am looking forward to our future projects.

Thanks to Lil Barcaski. a publisher with heart and passion, and someone who opened a door for me to share my heart with the world.

Last, but certainly not least, I'd like to thank my family for all the love and support they continue to give, even when they don't fully understand my need to write every day.

~Mattie

About the Author

Mattie Murrey-Tegels has been "in the trenches" as a medical SLP around the world for over 25 years and has for the past four years has been an Assistant Professor in a CSD graduate program. If you ask her patients and students, one thing they will all remember is how much she loves her work!

Since she has stepped into her Assistant Professor and clinical supervisor position, she has been working hard to help students bridge the gap between class and clinic. Her websites, Fresh SLP, Badass SLP, and podcast The Missing Link for SLPs, focus on just that, as she strives her best to provide coaching and courses for new and transitioning SLPs. Her courses target the skilled intervention we provide as SLPs and also the professional skills needed to not only survive our careers but thrive in our careers.

She is a regular state and national speaker in her field and a speaker for National Alliance for Mental Illness. . She is also on the Executive Committee for MNSHA, her state SLP association, as the Future Professionals Committee Advisor.

She is a contributing author of two chapters of colleagues' books, has written and published one of her own books. Lessons in Becoming: 52 Weekly Inspirations & Reflections on How to Become the SLP You Were Meant to Be is her second book

She may not look like it, but she is an introvert, and when she is not actively working as an SLP, she is almost always reading, writing (writing over 1,000,000 words a year) or listening to amazing Chicago Blues bands. She's ridden motorcycles for many years and this past summer completed a 1,300-mile solo trip to the Badlands of South Dakota and Needles Highway. Her favorite activity of all though is climbing into a hammock to nap or having timeless conversations with friends and family.

www.ingramcontent.com/pod-product-compliance
Lightning Source LLC
Chambersburg PA
CBHW081325120626
46546CB00011B/3218